The Dikler and His Circle

The Dikler and His Circle

MARY COMYNS CARR

WITH A FOREWORD BY
LORD OAKSEY

Illustrated

J.A. ALLEN
London & New York

Published in 1979 by
J.A. Allen & Co. Ltd.
1 Lower Grosvenor Place
London SW1W 0EL

British Library Cataloguing in Publication Data

Carr, Mary Comyns
    The Dikler and his circle.
    1. Dikler, The (Race horse)
    I. Title
    798'.45   SF359.5.D/

ISBN 0-85131-341-8

Typeset by Inforum Limited Portsmouth
Printed in Great Britain by A. Wheaton & Co. Ltd, Exeter

FORWORD

By Lord Oaksey

It would be a grave exaggeration to say that THE DIKLER has always been one of my favourite horses. On at least two racing occasions I deeply regretted his presence in the winner's enclosure, feeling, to tell the truth, that the world in general and the racecourse in particular would be a better, happier place if he was pulling a plough, or doing some other form of hard labour.

But even at those moments I wanted PENDIL to win the 1973 Gold Cup and my feelings after that Whitbread are not too difficult to imagine. I have to admit that it all depended on your point of view. To any unprejudiced observer the big horse was simply doing what he did throughout a long, active and honorable career, and for most of it I admired him as much as anyone.

From the moment he first appeared in a point-to-point I doubt if THE DIKLER even bored a single human being (Darkie Deacon and one or two jockeys might disagree but they would mean another king of "boring"). He could occasionally infuriate, he could certainly terrify and he could sometimes disappoint even those who knew him best.

But above all he was exciting. Great size is not always desirable but in THE DIKLER it combined with equally great strength and a headstrong attitude to life to make a magnificently explosive, unpredictable mixture.

You might never be sure just what would happen next, but you could bet your boots it would be well worth watching.

For much the same reasons Mary Comyns Carr's book is infinitely well worth reading. It is a fond and colourful account of THE DIKLER'S highs and lows and of the devoted human accomplices who helped him to achieve them.

I thoroughly enjoyed it and although PROUD TARQUIN might not agree with every word, I think he would join me in wishing both THE DIKLER and his biographer the best of luck.

I should like to thank all those who gave up so much of their time to talk to me about The Dikler and in particular to his owner Peggy, Diana Fanshawe, John Honeyball, Chub Castle, Darkie Deacon and Ron Barry.

Contents

Introduction

The stallion Vulgan, sire of The Dikler, bred in France, did most of his racing there; when sent to England he was trained by John de Moraville for a Mr. Summerville at Frethorne Stables near Wantage. Although his temper was to improve with age, in those days he was very coltish; and one morning he bit his trainer's thumb practically in two, for which uncalled-for act he was very nearly gelded. Fortunately, the operation was not performed because this son of Sirlan, out of Vulgate, was to become the greatest National Hunt sire of all times, and when the 1973-4 season ended in June he had been the champion sire of winners ten times. No champion in this century has got near such an achievement; and in the last, only St. Simon came near challenging it, being champion under rules nine times and, like Vulgan, gathering seven championships consecutively.

The turf record of Vulgan in France was excellent. As a two-year-old he won the Prix de Newmarket at Longchamp, and as a three-year-old the Prix de Northeast at Saint Cloud and the Prix Major Fridolin at Longchamp; and although he was placed second in the Prix du Cadre, again over $10\frac{1}{2}$ furlongs, he dead-heated for first place in this race and only lost it on a technicality. In his third season's racing he displayed his true potential as a tough, hard, battling stayer by winning the $1\frac{3}{4}$-mile Prix Filibert de Savoie at St. Cloud.

After crossing the Channel, Vulgan distinguished himself in his new country by taking the Queen Alexandra Stakes at Royal Ascot, which, being run over $2\frac{3}{4}$ miles, is the longest flat race in the British calendar; and he added to this victory in the Sunninghill Park Stakes, also run at Ascot, producing a great turn of speed to beat the favourite, Bayeux 11 (the best horse bred in Belgium for a number of years), in the final furlong.

As a six-year-old, when he gained another success in the

Valiant Stakes at Hurst Park, he was described in *The Sporting Life* as one of the best stayers to have come from France for several seasons. He won his only race over hurdles at Cheltenham in 1948. This was the Gloucester Hurdle, which has often been a stepping stone to fame. And there is little doubt that, had he continued his racing career, he would have won some major races over fences. In retrospect, of course, this would have been taking too much of a risk with him, since his value as a sire of jumpers far outweighed anything that he might have accomplished on the racecourse.

A year after winning the Valiant Stakes at Hurst Park, Vulgan made another bid for the Queen Alexandra Stakes, but was foiled of a double when beaten in a thrilling finish by Alindrake; and when he finished his racing career at the end of the 1949/50 season, after racing continuously for five years, he had won or been placed 12 times from 13 starts in England, while his total winning stakes in France amounted to 886,725 francs.

It has been said that, while there is no sure road to success in breeding steeplechasers, there do seem to be certain precepts in the pedigrees of high-class horses which, if followed, may at any rate help to avoid failure. The pedigree of Vulgan is linebred to Hampton in the direct sire and tail female line, and then combines six crosses to St. Simon and three crosses to Flying Fox. Sir Nigel, the sire of Sirlan, was a son of the triple crown winner, Gainsborough; while Laniste, Sirlan's dam, was out of Loetitia, one of the most famous of French stayers. Vulgate won eight races and was by Motrico, twice winner of the Prix de l'Arc de Triomphe and one of the most fashionable sires in France; while her dam, Vodka, was by Sans Souci, whose influence on breeding in that country was as well known as that of Blandford in Ireland.

Sirlan was retired to stud at the age of six after winning nine races, and he sired many winners. The racing career of his son, Vulgan, had proved that here was a sound, game, high-class stayer; and when he was sent to the Newmarket Sales, the British Bloodstock Agency bought him for Mr. F. Latham, who owned the Blackrath Stud in Co. Kildare. The price paid was £10,000, for the Irishman was looking for a horse of proven stamina who was, above all, a compact and agile sort. He thought that this kind would pull together the big rangy Irish mares and give them more quality – which is what did happen in a great many cases.

Vulgan's progeny were able to mature early enough to win on the Flat and yet were sound enough to reach the top under N.H. rules. At the start of his long career at the Blackrath Stud, Vulgan was considered by breeders to be too small at 15.3 h.h. (though his high withers made him look 16 hands). His new owner was told that Vulgan was more suited to sire harness horses than jumpers, so the first mares sent to him were of poor quality. To begin with, the covering fee was only £43.1 shilling; three years later, in 1954, Mr. Latham put it at 46 guineas and one guinea for the groom. Eventually it was to rise to 250 guineas, a record for a N.H. sire; and among the 775 mares covered by Vulgan in 17 seasons was a big handsome daughter of Grand Weather, winner of the Irish 2,000 Guineas and also a winner in the ring at the Dublin Show. This horse was the unraced Coronation Day, who was owned by a farmer named Moorhead; and it was Coronation Day who produced the big, strong bay colt who one day was to become known far and wide as The Dikler, one of the most brilliant and controversial steeplechasers of the century.

Neither mother nor son stayed long with the farmer. The mare was sold at Ballsbridge for £200, while the foal was bought for £500 by a dealer, Charlie Rogers, who had once managed Dorothy Paget's Irish interests.

Certainly Vulgan had proved a wonderful investment for Mr. Latham, having averaged over a winner a week season after season; and he retained his quality and zest for life till the end. "What sort of a temperament had he when he lived in Ireland?" I asked his owner. "Very good," I was told. "He was a nice kind horse. I had him for 18 years, my children grew up with him, and he was like one of the family." Mr. Latham then went on to say that Vulgan was also very game, afraid of nothing, and intelligent – qualities which he was to pass on in full measure to the subject of this book.

Chapter 1

THE DIKLER IS SPOTTED IN IRELAND

TWENTY-FOUR years before The Dikler was foaled, Edward Bee, the man who was to acquire him, returned to England from Africa. He had gone out to Rhodesia before the First World War because he wanted to farm, his father having got through all his money and left none for his sons. Growing maize in the Mazoe Valley in the 'twenties proved so profitable that when Edward Bee returned home he was able to rent the Cotswold Stud at Lower Slaughter in Gloucestershire which he ultimately bought; and although there was no resident stallion, he generally had eight to ten brood mares with followers, besides several high-class hunters. He had enjoyed his life in East Africa, where he had been joined by his brother, Ernest. Being interested in all sport, he had often gone big game hunting, though the first time he went into the bush he had been disconcerted to find that he was expected to pay a deposit on his potential funeral expenses, a precaution insisted upon by the authorities, since so many men were killed on safari. He was assured, however, that he could claim it back if he returned safe and sound.

A tall, well-built man who could have played cricket for his county had he stayed long enough in England, and no mean footballer, Edward Bee became extremely popular in Gloucestershire, for he had time for everyone, from dust-men to duchesses. A widower with no children of his own, he was very fond of his brother's two daughters, who had been born in Rhodesia. But only the elder one, Peggy, shared his love of horses. So she saw more of him than Katherine. He bought her a hunter and they would some-times go to meets together. "He was like a father to me after my own father died," Peggy recalls. Since he neither drank nor smoked, and lived very simply – he was a one-car, one-suit man – neither the years nor increasing weight diminished Edward Bee's amazing energy for farming (500 acres) and hunting. And it was in the hunting field that he first met Richard Fanshawe, late of the 12th Lancers and a fine rider who had been round Aintree more than once, besides being a team bronze medallist in the Three-day Event at the Berlin Olympics.

At that time Richard Fanshawe was Master of the Cotswold; and when he went to live in Lower Slaughter he and Edward Bee became firm friends. They would often play tennis together, another game in which Edward excelled. Never a social person, in that he did not go to, or give, parties, Edward was nonetheless delighted when Richard married the former Diana Ransom, fifteen years his junior. Especially when he found out that this attractive new partner on the court understood breeding to the same extent that he did. Diana's father had once owned the Lambourn Stud, and the breeding of racehorses was one of her strong interests. She was also a keen and highly successful point-to-point rider, winning the Cotswold Hunt ladies' race three years running on Scarlet Lancer and also the North Cotswold ladies' race in three successive years. So it was not long before Richard, Diana and Edward were going to race meetings together; and Richard and Diana would sometimes accompany Edward to Newmarket, where he sold his yearlings.

Yet while he bred for the Flat, the owner of the Cotswold Stud had steeplechasers as his hobby. He raced because he enjoyed it; though he was always thrilled when he won, Diana says. He had owned some useful N.H. horses, such as Limb of the Law and Bob Tailed Un, but he had not had a N.H. horse in training for some time when he decided to buy an annuity in the 'sixties. Most people do this to safeguard the evening of their lives. Edward had other ideas, and made no secret of the fact to his relatives that he intended to spend some of this money on restocking his stables with jumpers.

He had often crossed the Irish Sea to buy young stock, for

most of the best jumpers come from the Emerald Isle. There are several reasons for this. Though the fields over there may be casually fenced round, there are minerals and limestone in the soil, while the grass is kept free from artificial fertilisers; also it is in such fields that horses during their early years jump over little dykes and up onto banks to graze better grass, and thus begin to learn balance and to use their hocks. Captain Charles Radclyffe, the man who bought that outstanding hurdler Dramatist as a three-year-old, and a well-known figure at Irish sales, has said he has found that Irish horses destined for jumping learn much more quickly than flat-race horses do when being broken in.

It was in Ireland, therefore, that Edward Bee wanted his horses bought; but he wanted someone else to choose them for him this time. It so happened that the Fanshawes had decided to take a house in Co. Carlow for a year, as Richard, having been born over there, still had many relatives scattered about the country. Edward waited until the time came for them to say goodbye before telling them about his annuity. Then he said to Diana, "If you see two unbroken three-year-olds that you like, let me know and I will come straight over."

There was a saying in Gloucestershire, "If a horse is good enough for Di Fanshawe it's good enough for me;" and Edward Bee, no mean judge of a horse himself, had the highest opinion of Diana's judgment. Diana will tell you that what she looks for in a horse is "good depth for heart room, good shoulder, good hind leg, straight and strong, good inner thighs (very important), great length from hip to hock, good feet." And to this she adds, "I love big ears." What she doesn't like is "a horse who is narrow through the throat, narrow between the eyes and with long straight pasterns." Needless to say, to be asked to do something that she enjoyed, and could do really well, gave her great pleasure.

As soon as the Fanshawes had settled in their temporary

home, they motored up to the Ballymacoll Stud in Co. Meath to see what the late Charlie Rogers had to offer. Charlie Rogers was the man often referred to by Dorothy Paget as 'Romeo.' He had known that eccentric millionairess very well, and was one of the few people who got on with her without any trouble. Since her death he had built up a high reputation as a dealer; and indeed was said to have more good horses pass through his hands than any other dealer in Ireland.

Diana had not met Charlie Rogers before. "I was amused," she says, "to see that the gates were still painted in Dorothy Paget's racing colours." Richard, however, had known him in the hunting field, and Charlie was delighted to see him again. Diana, in fact, was looking for a mare by Vulgan for herself, and had seen one she did not want to buy. Walking on round the yard she suddenly said to Charlie, "Who is that horse looking over the door?" Charlie, believing that she was still thinking in terms of a mare, answered, "Oh, nothing that would interest you; he is a three-year-old by Vulgan."

Chapter 2

UNWANTED INHERITANCE

AMONG Vulgan's numerous progeny was a handsome gelding named Foinavon. Something of an eccentric in the equestrian world, he was described by one of his trainers as the laziest horse he had ever had in his yard. Certainly the unsaddling enclosure saw Foinavon seldom – in 22 races in Ireland he was to win only three; and if his new owner and trainer expected him to do better over the courses in England, they were to be disappointed, for Foinavon demonstrated his dislike of exertion by being placed only five times in 24 outings there.

More often than not, Foinavon was content to be the backmarker; and instead of moving up at some stage of the race, he usually tailed himself off. Not surprisingly, he was perpetually among the also rans. It almost seemed as though he enjoyed being on his own in a race; and since he was not very fast, he often found himself galloping without any company. Even so, at least one of his Irish jockeys felt that he could have been more successful if only he had had some ambition.

A famous Event rider once said that a horse, as well as the rider, needs to have a competitive spirit in order to do well, and this was conspicuously lacking in Foinavon. As a steeplechaser, he performed as if he knew that he was not going to keep up with the other horses, let alone overtake them. So naturally he saw no point in making the effort. Various jockeys tried desperately to make him change his attitude, but their attempts were nearly always in vain. Yet it was this very predilection for galloping on his own in a race that was to prove an enormous advantage when he ran at Aintree in the 1967 Grand National.

Up to this time, Foinavon had not won for two seasons. His starting price at Aintree was 100-1; and so convinced were they that their entry had no chance at all, neither owner nor trainer had troubled to make the journey to Liverpool to see how he fared. Foinavon's young jockey, John Buckingham, had only been offered the ride three days beforehand, but between them the two were to make racing history.

The field that memorable day included several horses with established reputations. The favourite was Honey End, who had already won six chases that season and was being ridden by Josh Gifford; and among the other fancied horses were Red Alligator, with Brian Fletcher up, and Freddie, the ex-hunter chaser who was the pride of Scotland, having been runner-up for the race two years running. And as the field approached the 23rd fence it seemed more than likely that one of these would win. But the whole character of the race underwent a dramatic change when the riderless Popham Down, becoming tired of jumping without his jockey, ran down the fence, colliding with the luckless Rutherfords, who was in front at the time, and also bringing down Limeking and Different Class (the horse that was owned by the American actor, Gregory Peck). These four horses baulked 20 others. In the confusion that followed, horses were going in all directions, with their jockeys in pursuit; and before they could be remounted for another run at the fence, John Buckingham was able to steer Foinavon (who up till then had been idling along near the rear of the field) through a gap in the melée. Foinavon, being no worrier, was neither upset nor distracted by the extraordinary scene that was going on around him.

So the nine-year-old son of Vulgan galloped on, taking the next fences as he had done the previous ones, without hesitation in his own time. John Buckingham had no problem keeping him going. The nearest danger to him was now Josh Gifford on Honey End, who, like Foinavon, had kept out of trouble, and was gaining ground rapidly. But Foinavon never faltered, and went on to win by 15 lengths. Flying machine he may not have been; nevertheless, his time of 9 mins. 49.4 secs. was over three seconds faster than

the time recorded by the 1966 winner, Anglo, who had
carried the same weight. In the toughest and most exciting
of all races Foinavon had consequently shown himself to be
a true son of his great sire.

It was another unusual son of Vulgan that Diana Fanshawe saw in the yard at Ballymacoll; and with Edward in
mind, she said to Charlie Rogers: "Wait a minute, I may be
interested. Can we have him out?" The three-year-old
brought from his box for her inspection was very big, and
he had a most intelligent head. "As soon as I saw him,"
Diana said, "I thought he had the makings of a high-class
chaser, and he appeared to be quiet and sensible. At that
time he already stood 16.2 and the only thing you could
fault about him was that he was a little bit on the leg; but he
had great girth and would obviously let down with time. So
we asked Charlie Rogers if we could have first refusal, and
as soon as we got home rang up Edward, who promised to
fly over immediately to see the horse."

The Fanshawes met Edward Bee at Dublin Airport, and
took him back with them to Co. Meath, where, recalls
Diana, "he made a very thorough examination of my
choice. He did not say much at first, but after we had the
horse walked and trotted he was clearly very impressed.
We then discussed the price that was being asked, a matter
of £3,000, and Edward wanted to know if there was any
'slush' money to be paid on top of this, stating firmly that if
there were any back-handers to go out Charlie Rogers was
to pay them. We then went into the house for a drink, and
Edward told Dorothy Paget's 'Romeo' that the deal would
go through subject to the horse being passed sound,
adding that he would get his own vet, Geoffrey Brain, to
come over."

Edward Bee stayed two nights with the Fanshawes
before returning home; he still wanted a second three-
year-old – he preferred them unbroken, so that he could
have them about the place before they were sent away; but
Diana had not yet found another she considered good

enough, and when eventually she decided on an unbroken colt by Arctic Slave (a sire of many winners), Edward took the colt on trust.

The day the horses were vetted by Geoffrey Brain, the Fanshawes had gone to Dublin to do some shopping, and when they got home there was a message waiting for them from Peggy's husband, David August, to say that Edward Bee had died suddenly of a heart attack "and would we please cancel the sale if possible." This was not, however, possible. Both horses had been passed sound that morning and so the sale had to go through.

Edward Bee's death came as a great shock to his friends, and the Fanshawes were stunned by it. There had been no warning signs that there was anything wrong with his heart. Indeed, at his last medical check-up the doctor had passed him sound; while the vigorous life he continued to lead out of doors (even though in the house a cut finger was looked upon as a major disaster) didn't suggest that he himself had any recent worries about his health. On the morning of his death, he was about to exercise one of his hunters when he ran back upstairs to fetch a handkerchief. His housekeeper heard him fall. Did Peggy, the god-daughter who was so close to him, suspect anything? All she remembers is that five years beforehand he had rung her up and asked her to go and see him; and when she did so, he told her that he was concerned about the final resting place of his African trophies, some of which he hoped would decorate Rhodesia House.

After certain bequests, Edward Bee left the residue of his estate to his two nieces, Katherine Gregory and Peggy August; and among the horses were the two three-year-olds from Ireland. Since the girls wanted neither, they were immediately put on the market for the prices that had been given for them. But they had had a bad time after leaving their stables at Ballymacoll before they were delivered at the Cotswold Stud, having been held up by a ferry strike; and Vulgan's son was so terribly thin that when Diana saw him again she was shocked. "He seemed all ribs and knees," she said. Yet, because of his breeding, Peggy, who was running the property until it was sold, was convinced he wouldn't stay with them for long. "All the same," she said, "we did have terrible problems with him."

The first two people who came to view the Irish imports held out hope. Mrs. Henriques went as far as saying that she would have liked to take the two but her husband had said that she was only to buy one, upon which she quickly removed the three-year-old who was to be named Padouk, a beautiful-looking horse who was hardly ever heard of again. Then another lady, Mrs. Barnard, came to consider the ugly duckling who had been turned out with some cows, and she said she would buy him provided that he was passed by a vet of her own choosing.

"And he turned the horse down," said Peggy. "He suspected that there was something wrong with his wind and that he would have to be hobdayed. This vet lunged him and lunged him and lunged him, and I presume thought that he could hear a noise."

It was after that depressing day that Peggy August said to Geoffrey Brain, who had passed the horse sound in the first place, "What *have* we got here?" Brain replied, "I stand by my word that he is the best three-year-old that I have seen this season." Unfortunately, there was no one else present to hear him express this opinion, and it was the other vet's report that soon became widely known.

Geoffrey Brain, the country's leading expert on respiratory problems, lives with his wife and two young sons near Bourton-on-the-Water, and when I went to talk to him there he told me how much it had meant to him to lose someone who had been one of his first clients when he set up practice in the Cotswolds.

"Mr. Bee had no horses in National Hunt training in 1965, but then he suddenly decided to buy some more, and when Mrs. Fanshawe had found them for him I went to examine two three-year-olds. I believe that he had also been interested in the purchase of an older horse but did not buy him in the end because he and the owner could not agree on a price – which was a pity as the next year that horse won the Irish Grand National! The two I vetted were the good-looking one by Arctic Slave who was named Padouk and a big lean animal by Vulgan with wonderful straight action that had extension to go with it – he used his shoulder and his foreleg, whereas a lot of horses move from the knee. The genetic make-up of speed was there, the action was there; and later on there was great muscular power and the strength to drive that action."

Geoffrey Brain's wife, who is very knowledgeable about young stock, had gone with her husband to Co. Meath and had formed her own opinion of the two horses. "I liked the three-year-old who had been broken and could be raced fairly soon," she said, "while I thought the Vulgan one rangy and very backward, and considered that he would obviously need a lot of time before he set foot on a course. Yes, his action was smooth and flowing, but the most striking thing about him to my mind was how unlike a Vulgan horse he looked."

The morning after the Brains arrived home, Geoffrey was surprised that Edward Bee did not ring him up to hear his verdict. "He was a man of great method and timing, and when he wanted to speak to me he would always ring at 7.15 a.m., so when I saw my partner I told him that I could not understand why I had not heard from Mr. Bee. I then learned that he would never call me again as he had died the day before." Like the Fanshawes, Geoffrey could hardly believe this at first; it was too sudden, too unexpected, too sad, and he went about his work with a heavy heart. "Then I heard that after much delay those horses had finally arrived at the Cotswold Stud, and I went over to see them. Padouk looked all right and he was quickly snapped up, but the other was thinner than ever and had a skin complaint which made him look even worse; and he remained at Lower Slaughter until September. One offer was made for him, but the lady insisted on having him examined by her own vet. Then, to my amazement, I learned that he had been found unsound. I could not understand it. Vulgan horses have always been sound-winded – of all the horses I have examined over the years, these have shown little or no weakness in their breathing capacity, and I immediately contacted Peggy August to find out if she would like me to re-examine him. Since she had lost the only person interested in buying him, she said 'Yes, of course.' So I went over and, finding him perfectly sound, issued another certificate."

Peggy named the horse 'The Dikler', after a stream that bordered her uncle's estate; and Mrs. Barnard, who had had the opportunity to buy him, and nearly did so, said later that perhaps it was a good thing that she did not buy him because she didn't think that her heart would have stood the strain of owning such an exciting horse.

Edward Bee had told his stud groom, "I don't think that I shall ever breed a Derby winner but I may have got a Gold Cup winner," and he was prepared to give the unbroken three-year-old all the time that he felt that he deserved, since he was not seeking a quick return for his money. But those who came to look at The Dikler after Mrs. Barnard did not share his view. They did not think that the horse would be a good buy at any price, considering him too big, too ungainly and too immature. He would need too much time before he could be raced, they reflected, and went away without as much as a "May we think if over?" or "We will let you know." One trainer did, however, tell Peggy that he would like to bring his father back in the afternoon. The father duly appeared, but though Peggy ran the horse up and down for them, and let them see him in the field, they had no more faith in him than the others; and after their departure she did not hear from them again.

The Cotswold Stud was sold in September 1966 and the Augusts took The Dikler back to their farm at Burford, where Peggy put him in a field. He began to look better, though he was still ungainly because he had outgrown his strength. She wintered him at Signett Farm and became quite fond of him. But she was still trying to sell him; and for the next year he was always for sale. Would-be purchasers, however, were conspicuous only by their absence; and when John Honeyball, who was going to break him in, came to fetch him, and asked Peggy what it was she called him, he received the reply "Tuppeny, because he is only worth two pence. No one will buy him."

John Honeyball did a very good job with the unwanted inheritance, and the following February Peggy exchanged a little horse she had in training in order to let The Dikler take his place. "I could not afford two racehorses", she said, and by then I knew he was fast – he could always leave my hunters far behind when they galloped in the field, even one who had been raced."

But The Dikler was still owned jointly by Peggy and her sister; and Katherine, who had never been interested in horses and had two sons to educate, saw the horse only as a liability, and began to say more frequently than before, "We really must get rid of him." This view was strengthened when he gained a bad report from the yard he had gone to. So she suggested to Peggy that they send him to the Ascot Sales and take what they could get for him.

"I could not, and would not, agree to this," Peggy told me. "I informed my sister that if The Dikler went to Ascot I would go too, and buy him; so would it not be better to save the expense of transport and commission if I bought her out? She agreed, and received £1,500, which was half what our uncle had paid for him. From then on I was my own boss where the horse was concerned."

When The Dikler became famous, Peggy was often asked to go into partnership, but she never would; and from that day to this The Dikler has remained her sole property. Nor was she ever tempted to sell when she could have named her own price for him.

Chapter 3

THE DIKLER'S FIRST RIDER

JOHN Honeyball, who first rode The Dikler, has an instinct for communication with horses that is born of sympathy with them. Coming from a background far removed from the equestrian world, he fell in love with horses when he was in his teens; and after that never wanted any job away from them.

Breaking in young horses is an art in itself, but John Honeyball has also built up an enviable reputation for re-educating those who in later years need curing of undesirable habits; and it would almost seem as though there is no such word as 'can't' in his vocabulary. Realising that, while no two horses are the same, some are much more different than others, he has thought out for himself how each individual should be handled; and though his methods may be unorthodox, they have proved effective. Even with those no other rider cares to risk mounting, he will achieve an understanding in the end after he has spent hours in their box getting to know them, both on and off their backs; and he is a natural when it comes to doing the right thing with them. Only mentally disturbed horses have defeated him. One such nearly killed him. It happened when a girl asked him to find out what was wrong with her horse, who had been behaving in a very odd manner. After riding him a little way he remembered nothing more until he recovered consciousness. He says that if the day ever comes when he does not want to mount a strange horse, he will give up altogether.

Most vices, John considers, are caused by human error; and he cites wrong girthing as the cause of much trouble. While firm in his view that a horse should not dominate a rider – "you must," he says, "be the master, so that they know who is going to manage them, and not the other way round" – he does not enforce mastery over them, and thus provoke them to resist. Instead he treats them as friends and allies, and by doing so wins their trust and confidence so that they do not look upon people as enemies. One horse who passed through his hands was a ferocious animal bent not only on eliminating his rider, whom he hurled to the ground on every possible occasion, but on attacking everyone who came near him with his fore feet. Such behaviour did not worry John. He expects problem horses to do unusual things; and today that horse is jumping on the Continent, having been sold after a successful performance at the Horse of the Year Show, where he had been ridden by Sue Honeyball.

It is through treating horses with consistent friendliness that John Honeyball is able to take them into society at an early date. As one owner explained, "They are so surprised at finding themselves in the hunting field or show-ring that they behave themselves." John agrees, and says that when a horse has to find an extra leg, display his paces in front of spectators, or get up out of a ditch, he is so busy concentrating on what he is doing that he has no time to think about playing up.

Of course, some of the horses John is entrusted with take longer to socialise than he hoped they would. But the end result is almost always the same; and in his wife John has found the perfect partner, for Sue Honeyball is not only a good show jumper, which in itself requires a high standard of horsemanship, but has the great advantage of being blessed, like her husband, with nerves of iron. Just as well, since she is often asked to walk immediately in front or behind a new horse he is schooling. And both of them would agree with Xenophon, the great Greek soldier, horseman and author, that never to lose one's temper is a good precept and an excellent habit.

John Honeyball was born in London, where his father was a quality surveyor for the Greater London Council; and while Mr. Honeyball Senr. was not interested in horses, he was fond of cats and dogs. John had no interest in school

Clive Hiles

John Honeyball on The Dikler at Buscot Show July 1968. No longer the ugly duckling, The Dikler was growing to look more and more like his dam, the handsome Coronation Day.

except to leave; and after he had failed the 11 plus, his despairing parents sent him to a private school, where the masters were more concerned with teaching him good manners than in turning him into a scholar.

When he was sixteen, John spent a month with a family in Cornwall who had a pony; and after harvesting he would go out riding, which he loved. Returning to Croydon, John soon realised, as did everyone else, that he was not going to get his school certificate, and decided that the only way to be reunited with horses was to work on a farm. "The teachers," he says, "ridiculed this idea. Most pupils wanted to be doctors or architects, but my brother had discovered *Horse and Hound* in a newsagent's, and in it was a list of shows. I used to bicycle out of Croydon to the nearest ones to watch the show jumping." He would leave his bicycle in a wood; and as he could not afford the money to go through the gate, he followed the fence round until he found a place in it that he could crawl through. Alan Oliver and Pat Smythe were often the big names at these shows, and John was fascinated, "though chiefly by the horses." He longed to be able to ride really well, but little thought that he ever would.

John's father, who had been very fair over the farming idea, suggested that he went to the local library to read the *Farmer's Weekly*, which advertised jobs. "But," says John, "the only sort of person who would have taken me required payment, and as I had often helped him with jobs my father considered that I was capable of earning my keep." His opportunity came when he saw an advertisement by the Y.M.C.A. for 'British Boys for British Farms', a scheme used a lot in London at that time, and which, since they were strict Baptists, his parents strongly approved of. The boys were sent to East Grinstead, where they did all sorts of duties with various animals so that the authorities could assess the type they would be best with.

"I wanted a farm with grass," John said, "as there would be more chance of horses being there. So I asked for a mixed one, and I was placed near Basingstoke in Hampshire." He was lucky in his employer, for Percy Horton was a great hunting farmer and he started the boy off riding round the cattle. "He did everything to encourage me," said John, who rose at 4.45 every morning to milk the cows, and after breakfast was kept busy with general farm duties. "But then one day Mr. Horton gave me a chestnut filly by the premium stallion Joyboy to prepare and take to an in-hand show, and she came third in a hunter class. After that she was due to go away to a famous horse breaker; but there was a long wait because he was so full up, and I was so certain that I could break her in that I put tack on her in the box and then lunged her. Though Mr. Horton seemed surprised, he made no objection when he saw me riding her about the place. The filly did go to the trainer in the end but he must have had an easy time with her."

That happy life in Hampshire was interrupted when John was called up to do his National Service; and while he does not regret the years spent in the Army, he still describes the first weeks as awful. At the end of two months he went before a Brigadier who was determined to get him into the Catering Corps, "because everyone except me wanted to be a driver. The Brigadier obviously did not like horses and was sarcastic when I suggested that I should go into the King's Troop or, as second choice, the R.A.S.C. Fortunately, I had a letter from our M.F.H. which said that I was eminently suited to work with horses, and though he tried desperately to persuade me to become a camp cook – it seemed that there was a shortage of them – I insisted, so he dispatched me to the King's Troop at St. John's Wood which was commanded then by Colonel Frank Weldon." John reckons he went to the barracks at St. John's Wood during the best period there has ever been there. "Colonel Weldon was a wonderful rider. He has won the Badminton Horse Trials, the European Championship, and collected an Olympic gold medal; and every evening I would creep up the stairs to the balcony overlooking the Riding School to watch him and Major Jim Russell, who was helping him with his dressage."

During John's second year in the Army there was a particularly difficult remount horse, and when the equitation sergeant realised how well Trooper Honeyball could manage him he was given permission to take the horse out on his half days off. The pair invariably went to Hampstead Heath, where they jumped benches not occupied by courting couples and John could dream about hunting.

After he had finished his time at St. John's Wood ("I didn't like the bull," he said, "but it did me good") he went back to his kind friend Percy Horton until he considered that he could make a living buying and selling ponies. His father was willing to give him a little help, so he rented some stables in a nearby village; but forage bills during two bad winters were high, and when he owed his father £150 he realised that he could no longer afford to be independent. Instead he went off to the Cotswolds to work as a valet chauffeur groom to Captain Charles Smith-Bingham. At that time the Captain had a large farm at Westwell, near Burford, and also owned superb hunters, since he was a keen follower of the Heythrop hounds. John lived in a comfortable furnished cottage and found himself laying out and brushing clothes ("the staff complained that I took straw upstairs on my boots"), driving cars and bringing on young horses which he showed in summer. During the hunting season he acted as second horseman three or four days a week. It was then that he came to the conclusion that he could earn some money breaking in horses during his spare time when the evenings were light. "Captain Smith-Bingham was very kind and let me use one of his cattle yards which had a box in the corner. I found a dealer who would give me £10 a horse, and after the first they came regularly."

Peggy August had been the first person hunting with the Heythrop to say "Good Morning" to John when he went to live in Oxfordshire. They became friends and often went riding together when out exercising. John did some work for Edward Bee, whom he describes as "a wonderful gentleman," and after his death Peggy took him over to the Cotswold Stud to see the remaining three-year-old whom she and her sister had inherited. John's first impression of the horse he came to know so well was that, although he was thin, he had very good limbs. "I did just wonder, though, where you put the saddle, as his withers seemed to be so far back. Mrs. August took the horse to her farm and fed him up that winter, and I remember that he was often kept in a big barn with other young horses. In the spring she asked me to break him in, as I was still living near her. At that time, Captain Smith-Bingham had not yet bought the Attington Stud at Tetsworth where I was to be his stud groom."

The first day John had The Dikler, Peggy August went over in the evening to find him riding the horse round the yard with a bran sack in place of a saddle. The four-year-old was very friendly and showed no bad temper at all. "Three weeks later," says John, "we went out riding together. A friend had some gallops, and we would trot round and then go over the training fences. The Dikler was turned out in the summer, and in the autumn there was no hunting for anyone owing to foot and mouth disease. Not that the horse was going out with the hounds at that time. When The Dikler returned from his unsuccessfull spell in a training stable, I received an S.O.S. from Mrs. August asking me if I could talk my boss into allowing me to take the horse back again. We had now moved to Tetsworth, and though Captain Smith-Bingham did remark that this was a stud, not a training stable, he said that he could come."

John has a vivid memory of what happened next. As soon as his owner had departed, he put a saddle and bridle on the horse (who he says was in very good condition) to find out what was supposed to be wrong with him; but when he mounted, The Dikler was frightened by something and, putting his head in the air, bolted down the long drive. John thought his last hour had surely come, for the road outside the gate used to be a very busy one before the motorway was opened; and he was just preparing to meet his Maker when The Dikler, who has always had a strong sense of self-preservation, heard the sound of the lorries as they sped past the gate, and put the brakes on just in time before he and John got among them. He then turned and bolted back up the drive, to pull up on the brink of the pond. "After that," says John, "I got off and led him back to a quiet little paddock and put draw reins on him – these go from the centre of the girth between the front legs to the bit and through a ring to your hands, so that when pulled they incline a horse's head downwards. You can only use them with a snaffle, though."

John rode The Dikler in these draw reins for a fortnight. He then changed the snaffle for a double bridle and took The Dikler to a local show, where he won a novice hunter class under Harry Tatlow, whose son, David, who is as well-known in the show-ring as he was as a point-to-point rider, wanted to 'produce' him. "But," says John, "Peggy was kind enough to leave him with me as I was growing more and more attached to him. I have never sat on a horse quite like him, and my only idea was to do what would be best for him. Since Peggy did not mind what I planned for him, some days he would go round a point-to-point course, as, with due respect to his late trainer, we had to find out that he *was* a racehorse; and then we would go to some more shows where quite often he would bring home a prize for looks and jumping. Once I took him to a show near London where he was entered for a riding-horse class; and the judge, who was a lady, evidently thought that it would be best not to mount him herself as he was so big and powerful. She had originally pulled us in first, then put us down a place. The following week her husband went with her to another show where again she was judging, and The Dikler and I were there too. I shall always think that her husband *dared* her to ride him, for she came into the ring with a hunting crop. Yet when she did get up on him she actually enjoyed her ride and we were presented with a silver cup."

Hunting might have been especially invented for Peggy August's big horse, he enjoyed it so much. But the first time John took him out cubbing with the South Oxfordshire it hotted him up. "I realised then," said John, "that the Thame Show was only a week away and I thought, Oh Heavens, with these manners it will be chaotic! In fact, he behaved quite well. The judge on that occasion was John Webber, and we won our class and The Dikler ended up Reserve Champion. Raymond Brooks-Ward was the commentator; and when it came to the Grand Parade, he announced, 'This is The Dikler; I gather that he is destined for the racecourses and we shall hear more of him in the future.' " Prophetic words.

It so happened that John was going through a difficult time in his private life, as he and his first wife had separated, but he told me that in moments of depression a ride on The Dikler was a real tonic to him. "He was so gay and full of life, and the most comfortable horse imaginable because of his beautiful conformation, balance and the way he used himself." (Geoffrey Brain says that they are both extroverts and that they clicked, just as some people do the first time they meet.)

Peggy paid John's hunting subscription with the South Oxfordshire because she wanted him to really hunt the horse and not just dawdle along at the back of the field popping him over an occasional fence. John says: "Although I was still a comparative stranger in this part of the country, I was asked to go on and assist the huntsman. I personally think that the Master would rather have had The Dikler in front where he could see him than gassing about behind him, for if he was kept in the rear of anyone he fussed unceasingly because he felt thwarted, whereas in front he relaxed."

One morning John was sent to the far side of a covert in

which there was some boggy ground. "There was a hedge in front of it and the quickest way into the wood was over it; so I jumped, forgetting the pitfalls I had been warned about. Brown leaves covered the ground, and my horse was soon up to his belly in mud. He struggled on through the slime – there was no panic and I was urging him along when suddenly we came to an enormous pile of wreathes and crosses. I couldn't even see the top, but he clambered up and next we found ourselves on a beautiful lawn with flower beds. We were in a crematorium! Although covered in slime, The Dikler walked sedately to the main gate, and just as we got there a hearse turned in and the horse stood as though to attention while I removed my hat. After that we slipped out, but it was quite an experience for him. And for me."

Boxing high-powered horses can be a problem, and The Dikler was no exception to start with. It took John three-quarters of an hour to get him into Peggy August's trailer when he started to go to shows. Yet as soon as he was provided with a Rice rear and front and side trailer he went in with no trouble at all, and he loved to look out. But John did have one failure with him during his time at the Attington Stud in 1968. This was when he tried to make the horse carry a side-saddle. During that summer a neighbour put on a show with a side-saddle class; and as she was worried that there would be insufficient entries for it, John told her that if she would like him to he would enter 'Tuppeny'. "I borrowed a habit and saddle, but alas got no further than putting the latter on, as he would not stand for the balancing strap – it seemed to drive him crazy and he put me on the ground so many times when I tried it on him that I had to give up."

Although The Dikler would have nothing to do with a balancing strap he has always been fond of children, and even during the week before he ran in his first point-to-point he was quiet with them. For it was then that John took him to work at an indoor school belonging to a friend, and one evening the owner brought her seven-year-old daughter along to watch. The little girl was very taken with the massive horse and begged John to put her up on him. "All right," he agreed, "and I will lead you," but she insisted on riding him by herself and, in her mother's own words, "The Dikler behaved like the gentleman that he is."

"I always knew that it had to come after he had done so well in point-to-points," John told me when he was talking about the decision to send The Dikler to be trained at Lambourn. "Peggy let me have him back every summer, and one year I took him to a Pony Club camp where I was helping. He lived happily in a little box and used to lead the way on cross-country rides and over suitable fences and ditches."

In the course of a conversation she had with me last year, Peggy said that had she the time over again, and had known what her horse was going to achieve, she would still have sent him to John in the first place; and at a party that she and Fulke Walwyn gave for the stable lads at Saxon House after The Dikler's triumph in the Cheltenham Gold Cup, John Honeyball was the only outside guest invited to the Malt Shovel Inn.

The Old Berkeley Point-to-Point in March 1969 was The Dikler's third point-to-point. Ridden by Captain Brian Fanshawe, he won the Open Race, beating the very useful Muck Orchid

Chapter 4

THE DIKLER IN POINT-TO-POINTS

POINT-TO-POINT races were designed for hunters carrying hunting weights and ridden by hunting men, and they started by being races from one point to another over natural fences. There would be an occasional turning flag to steer riders over a better line of country, and still later these were used to bring them back to the start so that spectators at least knew who had won, for in those early days courses were not made to suit the public. The type of horse has changed noticeably over the last fifty years. At one time winners in all open point-to-point races would probably have cost round about two hundred pounds; today the prices can easily run into four figures (sometimes more), and whereas half a century ago it would be good, bold hunters who made up the bulk of the entries, today many famous steeplechasers have graduated from point-to-point racing.

Since various claims have been made as to when the first point-to-point meeting was held in the last century, it is difficult to give an exact date. While the Master of the Atherstone in the early 1870's seemed certain that he was one of the first Masters of Hounds to have an annual point-to-point meeting, in a history of the Worcestershire Hunt compiled from original sources, and quoted from by Michael Williams in his book *The Continuing Story of Point-to-Point Racing*, Thomas Quarrell tells us that the first Worcestershire Hunt Meeting was on March 2nd 1836 over a course on the west bank of the Severn, and that the race was won by Captain Lamb's Vivian ridden by Captain Becher. Other meetings run by the Worcestershire Hunt were held up to 1864. Then there was a pause for nineteen years. Quarrell gives this description of the 1883 race: "The Meeting was attended by an enormous crowd of people mounted, who rode alongside of and behind the competitors, with the result that much confusion occurred, and Mr. E. Woodhouse, the Judge, had great difficulty in deciding the winner of the Red Coat Race and ultimately the result was given as a dead heat between Messrs. F. Lort Phillips and R.V. Berkeley."

"When point-to-point racing came under the jurisdiction of the Jockey Club in 1969 a loophole was closed," writes Michael Williams. "Before weighing out, all riders were required to produce to the Clerk of the Course a certificate of eligibility signed by their Hunt Secretary. Failure to do this resulted in permission to ride being refused. The object of the regulation, in the words of the statement issued at the time by the public relations office in Portman Square, was 'to ensure that point-to-point riders are all regular hunting people and have paid their minimum hunt subscriptions before the start of the season.' " After describing this as "an admirable precaution which has effectively removed the temptation to engage riders with dubious qualifications," Michael Williams goes on in his book to name Sunarise, Touch of Tammy and Bill Shand Kydd's Musk Orchid as the three most successful point-to-pointers of the 1969 season. He then says this:–

"But the star that glittered brightest of all was The Dikler, and no one is going to convince me that this one isn't gold, though several attempts have been made. This enormously powerful six-year-old, who took such a prodigious hold that he had to be hunted in a double bridle, first appeared on a course in a division of the open race at Beaufort, where he finished second to Touch of Tammy. He then won an open race at Crowell in the fastest time of the day, and repeated the performance at Kimble, where even Musk Orchid was made to look like a second-rater. The Dikler's next, and last appearance of the season, was in the open race at the South Oxfordshire, his home meeting; and here, I regret to say, not even that accomplished horseman Brian Fanshawe could prevent him from running out. So, in a manner of speaking, Musk Orchid obtained his revenge. . . . It was a discomforting moment for those of us who believed that in The Dinkler we had seen one of the most exciting prospects ever to appear on a point-to-point course. But though we were sadder, we refused to be wiser. And in view of the eminence that The Dikler has attained since, who is now going to say that we were wrong?"

When the decision was reached to run The Dikler in point-to-points it was essential to engage the best person to ride him on his racing début. So Peggy August rang up Diana Fanshawe and said to her: "You have always been connected with The Dikler, so I should like Brian [Diana's stepson] to ride him." Brian Fanshawe was then Joint Master of the Warwickshire and, like his father, a brilliant horseman. He was delighted to fall in with Peggy's suggestion. But it didn't go quite as planned, because frost caused the cancellation of the Oxford University Bullingdon Club meeting, where The Dikler was due to make his point-to-point début. So he had to wait for an open race at the Beaufort, and by that time Brian Fanshawe was unable to ride him, as he had to hunt hounds. So Peggy turned to another first-class amateur, James ("Chub") Castle, who farms near Thame, and whom she had met when she and his sister were bridesmaids at the same wedding. She had seen him riding at shows and over fences and been struck by his beautiful hands. Here now is Chub's story of his experience with this son of Vulgan in the race that first brought him to the notice of the public, and can be said to be the beginning of a spectacular career:–

"I first saw The Dikler at a county show where I was stewarding. We had a good horse, Scrum Half, who had run in 23 point-to-points and won quite a few of them. He was a real old hero, but by then getting past his prime. I asked John Honeyball, who was riding The Dikler at that show, if he was for sale, as he looked a fine type of chaser, and heard that he had been; but John was not sure whether he still was. However, as the horse looked as though he needed two more years, I didn't bother about him any more.

"The Dikler qualified for the 1969 point-to-point season hunting with the South Oxfordshire; and as I was also hunting with this pack, I was interested to see how he was going. Well, when you saw him cantering along with a field of hunters, it was very apparent how different he was from the others. We had a mare, Quick Answer, who had won 11 point-to-points out of 16 starts. Yet out hunting The Dikler was the master of her. I did think, though, that he would be difficult to race, and that without suitable tackle you would be lost. I knew Peggy August through my sister – she can ride anything – and when I heard that her horse was going to run in a point-to-point I wondered who would be on him, and was told Brian Fanshawe.

"And then, on the evening before the Beaufort, the telephone rang, and I was asked if I would ride him, because Brian was not going to, after all. Although I was thrilled, I was also a bit worried, as I knew that the horse had been taken out of training; and from watching him out hunting it was obvious that he could be a handful. But, as I told Peggy, it would be great fun to see how we got on together.

"Brian Fanshawe was an old friend; and as he had schooled The Dikler once, I asked him how he went, as there was a rumour that he had no steering and no brakes. But Brian only said that he hung to the left and pulled – which I reckoned that I already knew. John Honeyball did not have a lot of point-to-point horses, so I took to the meeting a drop noseband, and a running martingale to buckle on the breastplate to give me a bit of extra help. Sure enough, when we got there John had brought him over from Tetsworth in a plain snaffle. So I asked him to put the drop noseband on."

Chub decided that he would deliberately go to the paddock a bit late, as he did not want his horse to hot up and get upset; but when the stewards complained that he was slow to appear he could not, of course, tell them that it was done on purpose. "You rode straight out on the course there; and I thought to myself, if I wrestle with him it will only result in a match between the two of us. So as soon as we got onto the course I let him go, and on a long rein. The start was about two fields away and he went like the wind. He kept throwing his head out, but I let him run for about a furlong. He was waiting for me to grab hold of it, and then we came to a piece of the course that was very steep downhill. I said 'Whoa, Whoa,' and pulled him gently; and when I did touch his mouth, I believe he was quite relieved. He was expecting it and he pulled back into a canter."

It was a high-class race, with Touch of Tammy ridden by Roger Guilding in it, and several other useful hunter chasers; and Chub remembers how another rider looked at The Dikler and asked, 'What on earth have you got there?' Chub replied, 'A maiden, first time out, I don't know how he'll go.'

"There were a lot of runners," continued Chub, "but they started off quietly, and we were near the back of the field. I kept him covered up, and when we came to the first fence he jumped it crablike with his hind legs coming down almost before his front ones. I hadn't shown him the fence too soon, so that he could not charge off, and he went into it with his head up, and was thrown off balance. It took him several strides to get properly balanced again."

Meditating about the race beforehand, his rider had made up his mind never to haul at The Dikler's mouth. He hoped that he would settle down and not go too freely. He was confident that the horse could jump all the fences, and that if he did make a mistake he would get away with it. When they came to the second fence he let him have a better look at it, and gave him a little nudge for reassurance. The Dikler responded by jumping it rather better than the first, though in much the same fashion. But it was not long before he was starting to overtake the tailenders.

Chub let him have a good view of the next fence from some way back. "He jumped it more or less O.K., and though it felt as though he was only cantering, we were moving up and up and I felt fine, for not only could I hold him, but there was a wonderful feeling of power under me; and since he was not going barmy, I did not bother to keep him covered up."

To Chub's delight, the horse was jumping better and better, and after the first circuit, they had hit the front. "All I had to do then was just to feel his mouth. If I had sat against him he would have crossed his jaw and gone where he liked. Generally speaking, you sit against a horse just to keep him balanced, and he soon learns to balance himself against your firm hold."

There did, however, come a time in the race when The Dikler was going too freely, while not actually running away. Chub didn't mind this, because they were going down the back straight. "None of the others had overtaken us, though I expected something to do so at any moment. I remember thinking *This really is a smashing horse*. Then coming to the third last he made a mistake and pecked badly on landing; and just as his front end was getting up, his hind legs slipped sideways and he almost sat down. However, he soon got himself organised and kept galloping on.

"I was afraid that he would blow up – in the paddock he had not looked fit enough to last out three miles in a fast-run race – and I didn't want to push him too hard. Naturally, your intention should always be to win, if your horse is good enough. But no one should give a young horse an unnecessarily hard race, especially first time out. That would only cause him distress."

At the second last, when Touch of Tammy, who was later to prove himself one of the top hunter chasers of the season, and wind up winning the *Horse and Hound* Cup at Stratford, loomed up alongside The Dikler, Chub realised that the best he could hope for was second place. The Dikler was now beginning to tire. "So," said Chub, "I just let him hack on at his own pace. I knew that if I tried to ride a finish he would not find anything more to give. I took a firm hold of his head to make sure that he did not fall at the last, and what happened then was very interesting, because the moment I did this he started to go to the left; but he jumped the fence all right and finished second." (The only photograph Chub has of this race shows him with all his weight on his right hand trying to keep The Dikler straight).

It was, of course, an outstanding performance, and Chub would dearly have loved to have ridden The Dikler again. Brian Fanshawe, however, had been promised future rides on the horse; and so this was the only date that Chub Castle and The Dikler had together. "At that time," says Chub, "my godfather, Harry Bonner, was managing General and Mrs. Mellon's steeplechasers, and I rang him up and told him about Peggy August's horse, and said that he might be for sale. Harry had seen him at shows and was not enthusiastic about him; so he did not find out if he was or not. The thing I shall always remember about The Dikler is how quickly he learnt – I honestly believe that you could have taught him anything."

But had The Dikler really been for sale then or not? I asked Peggy to clarify the situation. Which she did. She said that after she had bought him outright she gave up trying to sell him and no one approached her until three days before his first point-to-point, "when Jack Cann, who was one of the people who had been to see him as a three-year-old, but had said that he could not afford to have a horse waiting about for so long, made inquiries through Diana Fanshawe. After a lot of thought I decided not to sell then as it would so disappoint John and Brian who were all geared for his first race. Having turned down that inquiry, I think it was then I decided to be stubborn and stick by the horse. I was offered £8,000 for him after he had come second in his first point-to-point; and when he won his second I was offered more by another person. But I still said no; and after he came first in the Honeybourne Novices' Chase at Cheltenham in November 1969 I told Fulke Walwyn that he would never be for sale again." And Peggy stuck to her word, though later on amazing offers were made for the one-time derided bay gelding, from abroad as well as from patrons of the Turf in this country.

"Yes," said Brian Fanshawe, who rode The Dikler in his next point-to-point, "his jumping was always superb but he ran away like mad. He was very big and very fast and you got the impression that he had always been bigger and faster than the horses he met. He crossed his jaw, or at any rate it felt like it, so that you had no control over him. Yet I did not find him frightening to ride, probably because he was so intelligent. He would sweep up to a fence, having judged the distance a hundred yards away, and then adjust his stride to it."

While he was no trouble in the paddock before contesting his second point-to-point, Div. 2 of the open race for the Faber Cup at the Oxford University meeting at Crowell, when taken down to the start he carted Brian half a mile beyond it. Returning to join the others, he consented to stay with them when they set off and his rider tried to tuck him in. "Though after a while," said Brian, "I had to let him go, and once in front he settled down." He won the race by a distance in the fastest time of the day, and then circled the car park before pulling up. The only thing that troubled Brian that day, he remembers, was that he was riding in the next race and his wrists were numb. "No, he didn't fight you if you didn't fight him, but I have never been on a horse that leaned on you more. He was like a dead weight."

The Dikler's next race was in a division of the open event at the Old Berkeley meeting at Kimble, where he had Musk Orchid as his chief rival, and beat him by two lengths. "I let The Dikler go in front," says Brian, and though Musk Orchid never caught us, he got fairly close. For most of the race The Dikler never made a mistake, but over each of the last three fences he was trying to run out. Why did he want to do that? Well, he would be all right on the first circuit, but on the second he knew that if he cut out a fence he would be at the next one more quickly; and in his next point-to-point, which was also his last, he did run out."

This was the open race at the South Oxfordshire, his home meeting; and while he did run away when going down to the start, this time he pulled up when he got there, "as if," says Brian, "he knew what was expected of him." Unfortunately, there were several fences in a line at the end of the first circuit; and although The Dikler was bowling along well in the lead, and Brian managed to keep him straight until the final one, he ran round it. "There was a right-angle corner just after this fence, so he wanted to take a short cut into the straight, and he caught my foot on the wing and fractured my ankle. I might have gone on except for that."

"Brian never told me that he had fractured his ankle," said Peggy, "and I did not know about it until Diana informed me." But while he made light of the injury, Brian Fanshawe was convinced that the horse ought not to run in point-to-points again, because there were no running rails at them. He was all for The Dikler going to a professional trainer to run on racecourses where such rails are the usual thing, though he knew that there would always be a problem to get the right jockey for him. "He was a real character, and whenever Ron Barry and I meet we talk about him, because we are about the only people who rode him who have not retired."

In a letter to Peggy which I have permission to quote, Michael Williams, the point-to-point correspondent of *The Sporting Life*, wrote:–

Dear Mrs. August,

While I am extremely sorry that we shall not be seeing your splendid horse on the point-to-point courses again, I feel that you are doing the right thing with him and I am sure that he will win a lot of chases for you. Few horses have given me so much pleasure in point-to-points; Matchboard was another such last season, but she had not got The Dikler's magnificent looks. To see him parading round the paddock like a heavyweight ballet dancer was an absolute joy.

Chapter 5

THE DIKLER'S TRAINER

FULKE Walwyn, the man who trained The Dikler throughout the horse's career in National Hunt racing, has often
been described as the best trainer of long-distance chasers
in the world, and horses trained by him have won the
Cheltenham Gold Cup four times. He has also both ridden
(Reynoldstown in 1936) and trained (Team Spirit in 1964) a
Grand National winner. Born in Wales, where his father
was a Master of Foxhounds, Fulke grew up with horses,
and riding came as naturally to him as breathing. Once a
serving officer in the 9th Lancers, he was amongst the best
amateur riders of his day, as was his friend and brother
officer, the late Frank Furlong, who also won the Grand
National on Reynoldstown.

In 1930, when Fulke won the Royal Military Academy
(Sandhurst) lightweight race at the Garth point-to-point
meeting at Arborfield, Frank Furlong also rode a winner
there. Four years later, both riders were decanted at the
same fence in the Grand National when Really True clipped
the top of it and fell and Ready Cash came down trying to
avoid him. The following year, Reynoldstown, owned and
trained by Major Noel Furlong and ridden by Frank, came
home in front of Blue Prince; and in 1936, when Reynoldstown won his second National and Frank was unable to
ride him because of a weight problem, not even a lost
stirrup at the third last could prevent Fulke from scoring in
his place.

Frank Furlong, who was said to dislike hunting because
he liked to know what was on the other side of a fence, was
killed in action while serving with the Fleet Air Arm. Fulke
Walwyn, who had left the Army in 1936 in order to turn
professional, was forbidden by his doctors to race again
after fracturing his skull and being unconscious for a
month. So in 1939 he took out a trainer's licence.

From the beginning of his new career, Fulke showed his skill as an equine therapist, for some of the first horses sent to him were ones who had broken down; and it was through his care and patience that their legs were repaired and they were restored to racing. A genuine animal lover, he puts the welfare of the horses in his yard first; and his owners find that they cannot run them in a race until Fulke considers that they are ready to appear in public. Young jumpers are often ruined through being asked to do too much too soon; but at Saxon House, Lambourn, where Fulke Walwyn has his stables, training is never hurried. Fulke is brilliant at the strategic planning of a horse's career. His remarkable record is proof of what a great trainer he is. Not only has he won most of the major races in the jumping calendar, but several of them on numerous occasions. His success is due to a combination of knowledge, skill and total dedication (his only other interest is gardening). He has, too, a great feeling for those who work with him. There is a spirit of mutual trust and esteem in his yard, and tributes are spontaneous from those he employs.

Fulke is a perfectionist, and the stable lads at Saxon House benefit so much from the high standard he sets that nine out of ten of them could hold a position as head lad in most other training establishments. That, at any rate, is the opinion of "Darkie" Deacon, who had charge of The Dikler there. "Anyone who works for Mr. Walwyn," he says, "knows that he knows more than they do. Although he does not suffer fools gladly, he is a kind man, and people can say what they want to him. He always gets straight answers from me, and is not too proud to ask for an opinion."

Darkie's wife, Joyce, has known the trainer over a period of thirty years, as she first worked for him when she was seventeen. A cheerful comfort-maker whom anyone would like to have about their home, she goes up to Saxon House to help Fulke and Cath Walwyn whenever she is needed, and one gets the impression that she feels almost maternal towards him. "I have known Mr. Fulke for so long," she tells you, "that I understand his moods. I know not to commiserate with him if he has had a disappointment, and not to talk when he wants to be silent – trainers have many worries, even ones as successful as he is. But most of the time he is full of fun and very thoughtful to others."

Nick Gaselee, who was Fulke Walwyn's assistant for five years and now has a yard of his own, says: "If anything goes wrong he flies up into the air and lets forth. But it is over quickly and then forgotten. Unlike some people who work an error to death, everyone knows where they stand with him, and his staff seldom want to leave. His attention to detail is marvellous. He is so thorough that when he goes round the stables in the evening to give every horse a carrot, or something that they will enjoy, he will immediately notice if anything is amiss; and he is always interested to hear from the stable lads what they think of their charges. He is also a genius at being able to pick out a horse's true potential, by which I mean whether it is a two-miler or a three-miler, regardless of pedigree." Gaselee then went on to remark how much he admired the Master's ability to produce consistent winners from amongst the horses he had bought at a moderate price for other people.

Peggy August has this to say about how she came to send The Dikler to Saxon House to be trained: "Having written to The Dikler's previous trainer to tell him that my horse would not be returning to him, I was then faced with the task of choosing another trainer after the horse had run so well in point-to-points. One day Charles Radclyffe, who is a great friend of the Walwyns, asked us over for drinks to meet Fulke and Cath; and shortly afterwards, in May 1969, I arranged to go to Lambourn for evening stables to see the establishment, find out how Fulke liked things done, and whether I still felt that this was a place where I and my horse would fit in. I wanted it known that I intended to see the horse run in all his races, and that I would like to see him schooled whenever I could and be kept informed generally; though naturally I made it clear that I had no thought of interfering in any way in the matter of where he should run.

"I remember the day I went for my interview very well. It was the day that I had to have my favourite hunter put down. Ned was twenty years old and had carried me well for twelve seasons. When I went to say a last farewell I assured him that no other horse could give anyone so much fun. Little did I know! Having seen Saxon House, I agreed that The Dikler should go there in July. In the meantime, when the news got round where he was going, all the people who love gossiping told me that, though Fulke was a great trainer, he was crabby, and he really only had horses for the élite. So shouldn't I have second thoughts? But I felt committed, and that I must give The Dikler the chance he needed. Yet when the day came for John Honeyball and me to deliver him I went in fear and trembling, although Fulke had already said, 'I'll take him.' But would he make the grade? I was wondering. We drove through Lambourn with the Land Rover and trailer and when we passed a string of horses from Saxon House it was obvious from the expression on the lads' faces that my horse's reputation had preceded us."

Peggy knew that with such a complex horse there would clearly be ups and downs. "Not trainer against owner," she said, "but taking the rough with the smooth. Sometimes we were disappointed, sometimes baffled, and we would try to work out a remedy. Then at other times things were too good to be true. But through it all I can truthfully say that Fulke and I never had a cross word. Even when I insisted that the puckle be removed – a procedure which resulted in near-disaster – he just said, 'That's what happens,' and after a telephone call the subject was not mentioned again."

"I did not know much about The Dikler when he came here," Fulke told me, "though as soon as we got him we

heard certain stories, such as that he was mad and dangerous. But it was apparent that he was a very high-class
horse."

So many fine chasers had come to Saxon House to be
trained; and now here was one who was to give Fulke
tremendous pleasure, exasperating as he could be on occasions, the most extraordinary of all the outstanding horses
he had had in his yard, one who was to take his place
among the stars like Mill House and Mandarin. Fulke Walwyn has always liked big horses, and this one stood 17.2
h.h. Fulke also likes a challenge, and The Dikler provided
him with this from the outset, proving a law unto himself
when it came to training.

"He was a horse of whom you could never say, 'I'll do
this with him today,' " said his trainer. "And you could
seldom work him a mile and a half, only seven furlongs; he
always worked on his own over fences, as otherwise he
would start racing – as it was, he took them at about a
hundred miles an hour. Then, with a lead horse, if he took
it into his head to pass him he would soon be far in front
galloping flat out; but when he went too fast on the downs
he frightened himself by his own speed – it was the only
thing that did frighten him. Otherwise he was completely
fearless, and it took too much out of him. The next time he
went on the downs he would look at the gallops, and at
everything else; and he used to keep stopping, because he
did not want to gallop again."

Fulke Walwyn had ridden the famous Golden Miller in
two races after he turned professional; and he had been
Dorothy Paget's chief N.H. trainer after the War, winning
his first Cheltenham Gold Cup with Miss Paget's French-
bred Mont Tremblant, in 1952. That formidable lady had
soon found that Fulke did not intend to be woken up in the
middle of the night to hold long conversations about her
horses, as poor Basil Briscoe, her former trainer, had been
obliged to do. With tactful firmness, Fulke made her understand that there must be no calls after nine in the evening.

This was necessary, because the eccentric millionairess, being a compulsive eater, paid a cook to be on duty until 5 a.m.

A leading patron of the Turf – her horses won a total of 1,534 races – Dorothy Paget invariably appeared with her stout figure buttoned into a tweed coat which became nearly as well known in the 'thirties as Queen Mary's toques; and when she died at the age of 54 in 1960, the room above her bedroom was stacked to the ceiling with piles of sporting papers which she never liked to have thrown away. A difficult despot, though kind and generous to friends and those whom she felt deserved help, she still remains the only owner besides King Edward VII to have won both the Grand National and the Derby, the latter with a horse she bred herself, Straight Deal. According to Fulke Walwyn, Miss Paget's Golden Miller, hero of no fewer than five Cheltenham Gold Cups, was not really an Aintree type, as he jumped off his forehand – which caused him to dislike big drops. This makes his victory in the Grand National of 1934, when he carried top weight and won in record time, all the more remarkable.

The owner of Saxon House has kept his figure, and when he descends from the Land Rover accompanied by his beloved Scottie he looks more like an actor of the Rex Harrison school than a trainer, except for his legs, which are those of a horseman. Despite his extremely busy life, he creates an atmosphere of unhurried calm when he sits talking to visitors in his study, one wall of which is completely covered with photographs of horses he has had through his hands, with a coloured one of The Dikler occupying pride of place. Another great favourite, Mandarin, the horse on whom Fred Winter won the Grand Steeplechase de Paris of 1962 after his rubber bit had broken at the fourth fence of this four-mile race, the same year that he won the Cheltenham Gold Cup, is not far off.

Of The Dikler's jockeys, Fulke makes special mention of Willie Robinson, "who was very good with him and had the worst time of all of them because he rode him in his raw days; and yet he never seemed to have any trouble holding him. He rode him on a long rein and never fought him."

While Peggy August herself is not in the least superstitious, she found that her trainer was extremely so. So she was not surprised when, after the Whitbread Gold Cup of 1974, he said to her, "I knew we were going to win, as I have a new car and I have never been to races in it without having a winner, and yours was the only runner I had today." And she remembers how, at Wincanton, Fulke had to sit on his lucky coin, while at some racecourses he would stand in certain places against the rails because he had stood there before when horses from his yard had been victorious. Even the great have their idiosyncrasies.

Chapter 6

THE DIKLER'S LAD

PETER Willett once said to me, "Never be sorry for trainers, they get paid for doing what they like best." The same might be said for "Darkie" Deacon, who looked after The Dikler and Charlie Potheen and rode them out each morning while they were at Saxon House. Although riding headstrong tearaways over snow-covered downs may not seem such an enviable way to spend one's time as working in centrally-heated offices, Darkie finds these rides exhilarating, except when the wind is in the East, and he has demonstrated that it is not so much strength as knack that enables him to control such steeplechasers.

Born in Swindon, Darkie grew up in Wiltshire; and although none of his relations rode, he would mount any horse or pony that he had the chance to, and later was to enjoy some show jumping. Since he was very light, it seemed only natural to become a jockey after he left school, and he was duly apprenticed for three years to Ossie Bell's flat-racing stable in Lambourn. But Darkie, who is so nick-named because he has jet-black hair, had the misfortune to arrive there three months after a more experienced apprentice, Tommy Gosling. Naturally, Tommy got all the best rides; and though Darkie did have the odd one, he never had a winner.

After Ossie Bell retired, Darkie worked in several other racing stables. Yet whenever he looked like riding a winner for one of them something always happened to prevent it. Once, when he was due to ride a really good horse, Fairey Fulmar at Epsom, his mother died the day before; then there was a time at Chepstow on Easter Monday "when we were beaten by a neck as I had been serving in the Army as officers' mess cook until the previous Saturday – which was hardly the ideal preparation for a race."

Towards the end of the 'fifties, by which time Darkie was

Darkie Deacon holding The Dikler and Charlie Potheen in the yard of Saxon House, Lambourn.

married and had three young sons, lack of money made him take a job at Aldermaston; and since his family still lived at Lambourn, he had to travel 50 miles a day to it – which meant that he was away from home 12 hours out of 24. So he gave it up after 18 months. He then found himself out of work. But his love of horses was too strong to be denied and, with the backing of his understanding wife, Joyce, who has never been jealous of the part horses have played in his life, and knows how empty his world is without them, he went back into racing instead of looking for a better-paid but less satisfying job. He says he cannot quite put his finger on why he chose a jumping stable rather than a Flat one again. He did, however, have a friend who worked at Saxon House; and soon Fulke Walwyn, who never advertises for stable lads, sent down a message asking Darkie to go and see him. "I have been with The Guv'nor ever since," he says. "Of course, one of the reasons I have stayed is because his is a successful stable; but if I had not liked him as a person I should have gone ages ago."

If you ask this modest, friendly man what the secret of his success with horses that need special handling is, he will answer simply, "they know I like them;" and as horses of this sort were allotted to him before he came to Saxon House, it has never made any difference to him whether he rides these or those of placid temperament who can be relied upon to behave themselves on road and downs alike. And Joyce never worries about him after he has driven off in the morning. She has confidence in his confidence and is justly proud of his skill. Today one of their sons is a coach builder, another an electrician, while the youngest works for a saddler in Lambourn and once made a rubber bit for The Dikler.

In the sitting-room at No. 45 Woodland, where the Deacons live on a council estate, there are numerous pictures of horses and boys, the former outnumbering the latter by two to one. And you are shown the beautiful carriage clock which has simple inscription on it:

The Dikler
1969-1976
Darkie Deacon

This carriage clock was presented to Darkie by a grateful owner. Outside, the vegetable garden is well stocked, and the front beds show roses and dahlias in season, both the Deacons being keen gardeners. But for relaxation, Darkie, who has every other weekend off from Saturday noon to Monday morning, plus four weeks holiday a year, likes playing golf; while his other recreations are racing, reading and studying the form book – though he is not sure that this last preoccupation could fairly be termed a recreation.

Darkie remembers well how he came to look after the horse who, together with the black chaser Irish Imp, has remained his favourite. "The Guv'nor called me over one morning and said, 'I'd like you to do this horse. He has come with a bad reputation but I think he will be a good one as he has shown excellent form in point-to-points.' When he arrived, Mill House was still in our yard, and he was a big horse too. Yet once when we were out together, The Dikler put in a fly jump from a standstill and went clean over Mill House's hind quarters; but his balance was so perfect that I did not fall off."

In fact, Darkie rarely came off The Dikler (except twice when he reared); whereas Charlie Potheen, one of the kindest horses that Darkie has ever looked after, often put him on the floor when he dropped his shoulders and whipped round. Of this horse, Darkie says, "He looked only for sugar and sweets. At exercise he was full of high spirits and devilment but racing took a lot out of him – which was why he could only be raced lightly."

According to Darkie, Vulgan's progeny were highly strung; and if you took a son of his from A to B on the road and then turned to go back to A, "he would start to jog and get excited. When The Dikler first came to us, he would rear if he was held up, because he always wanted to go forward; and twice he came right over backwards, once in a lane and once on the road, but both times I jumped clear and was not hurt, and after a time he stopped doing it. He did, in fact, become much quieter. On the gallops he would get the bit between his teeth and he certainly could pull; but there again, Charlie was the more tiring of the two. The Dikler was such a comfortable horse that you did not mind him pulling – floating is the only word to describe his action, though even when walking he would dance about on his toes."

I asked Darkie what had been his first impression of The Dikler, and he replied that for the first day or so he thought that he was just a big boat. "He seemed so colossal, and

when I took him over to the indoor school at Seven Barrows
– where Mr. Peter Walwyn, the Guv'nor's cousin, has his
stables – he never stopped jogging for a moment."

"Had he a hard mouth?" I asked.

"No, a perfect one," answered Darkie, and went on to
say that when The Dikler was galloping he would hold his
breath – something that he had never known another horse
do. "And then," Darkie continued, "he would slow himself so that he could breathe again. We did not often school
him over fences, there was no need – in the first year three
or four times, and after that generally one time in a year.
Once when schooling with a jockey – not Stan Mellor – the
mist came down and he disappeared into it going flat out.
Horse and rider finished up on the White Horse Hill Gallops two miles away. Mr. Walwyn was very worried, as the
horse was due to run in a race the next day, and he sent
someone to look for him. They found The Dikler retracing
his steps. The next day he came second to Crisp in the Top
Rank Club Chase at Ascot."

Darkie is indignant that stories appeared in the Press
making out The Dikler to be a ferocious character, and
suggesting that his stable lad was in constant danger of
having some portion of his anatomy either chewed or
bruised. The Dikler, he says, was neither a tiger nor
malicious-minded. "Sure he would prance at you and grab
hold of your arm, but he did not mean any harm; it was just
his way of showing you who was boss in his box. I think it
satisfied his ego. When I opened his door in the morning he
was nearly always in a good temper and would trot over to
me to be made a fuss of. But when I went to put the head
collar on he would duck away; and although he almost
filled the box, he could cavort like a pony because he used
himself so well. He loved to play about before he went out
for exercise."

After Darkie had done the mucking out, he would put
The Dikler's tack on, using an ordinary exercise saddle.
"And he liked me to swap his bits around, so that one week

he would wear a snaffle, and another it would be a rubber bridle with a chain through the bit which a horse does not know is there but which gives a little extra strength for the rider. Nearly all the time I rode him on the roads it was in a bitless bridle – he had a very, very tender mouth, and it bled easily."

It was soon found that The Dikler also felt the cold, so much so that his stable lad took him out with the second string whenever possible when it was warmer. In winter, the horse wore three rugs; and when the weather was severe there were infra-ray lights in his box.

As I knew that The Dikler spent his summer holidays with John Honeyball at the Attington Stud, I asked when it was that he returned to Lambourn, and was told that it varied, but was usually August. The year before he won the Cheltenham Gold Cup, however, it was not until September. Peggy August says that The Dikler needed this rest from racing, and she liked him to have a good long time out. Darkie, on the other hand, makes no secret of the fact that, if he had had his way, he would only have left the horse out for six weeks. "He put on weight fast and I like to see a horse coming back from the field a bit light, because then all the work you do with him before the first race turns into muscle. Otherwise you have got to get the fat off first. It was not until February that I was really satisfied with The Dikler's condition," he added reflectively.

The Dikler needed nearly three months of road work, and Darkie would keep him out on average $1\frac{1}{2}$ hours to begin with, increasing this time to $1\frac{3}{4}$ towards the end of the period. From Saxon House the way to the downs is through Fulke Walwyn's paddocks to the top of the lane, after which horses walk along a tarmac road for about two furlongs and then beside a sand gallop until they reach the turf ones. When Darkie cantered The Dikler up there, the horse was always longing to gallop. "And though I did not always hold him, I generally could. When he did take off with me it would be because he was excited by something –

music from Peter Walwyn's indoor school, that would get him going – but I rarely had difficulty in pulling him up. And when he had frightened himself by going too fast he would tremble while he was being saddled up the next day. We worked him with the hurdlers, and even against a young one he was much faster; we would also work him with a flat-race horse named Spitzbergen who had been fourth in a race at Ascot, and my one could still beat him with ease over a mile."

When they came back to the yard, Darkie would wash The Dikler's legs if they needed it, and pick out his feet. Next he gave him his twelve o'clock feed, $2\frac{1}{2}$ bowls of oats (the head lad gave him his first feed of the day). The Dikler could get through the best part of 21 lbs. of oats when he was eating well after Christmas. Yet though he was an excellent feeder much of the time, he was a very dodgy one in fast work or when he was racing. The only things that he really liked then were Cox's Orange Pippin apples, and Darkie spent a pound of his own money every week buying these for him. He would grate them and mix them with the horse's feed. The Dikler, he found out to his cost, didn't at all care for Golden Delicious! Once, when Darkie could not get Cox's, he tried these out as a substitute. The horse knew at once that this was not his usual apple, and showed his displeasure by leaving them. "I never tried them on him again," said Darkie.

"The Dikler rolled a lot," Darkie went on to tell me. "He once got Mr. Walwyn out of bed at two in the morning when he got cast in his box. The head lad had to go and help to pull him away from the wall, by getting hold of his tail. The Dikler was also a scraper. He would scrape the floor of his box after I had tied him up at 4.30 p.m., staying that way until the Guv'nor came round the stables at six."

It seems that The Dikler was also very ticklish, and that his skin was so thin that even a rug could rub it sore. Never the easiest of horses to groom, he would jump about and kick out as Darkie pursued him with the body brush. But although it had taken three hours to clip him the first time it was done, he soon grew not to mind the electric machine; and he was so good to shoe that the blacksmith loved him.

At 6.30 The Dikler was brought his evening feed of oats and hay – nets are not used at Saxon House, so the feed is put down in a corner of the box. The supplements, when added, were glucose, damped bran, carrots, and vitamin E in powder form; and before Darkie leaves his horses for the night, he gives them two or three mint balls.

When I asked what The Dikler was like with car traffic when he was in training, I was told that he was perfect, but that he could also be a handful on the roads owing to his dislike of tractors; if one of these came up behind him, he would refuse to let it pass, diving out into the middle of the road to stop it. And if he became interested in anything, such as a man digging his garden or an aeroplane over-head, he was virtually immovable. Darkie says that he will always remember how The Dikler used to stand at the top of the paddock at Cheltenham gazing at Cleeve Hill.

"The only time The Dikler ever kicked me," Darkie reflects, "was on the afternoon that he won the Chel-tenham Gold Cup. Somehow I thought he would that year. His nerves were on edge. He was very fidgety after I had put on his racing plates the previous day, and I had just put his parade rug on when I received a kick on the thigh. He had never kicked me before, and he never did again. But once was enough. I was in such pain that I could not lead him before the race; and Tommy Turley, the travelling lad, had to do that. Fortunately, I was all right by the time he had beaten the course record and Pendil; and when we got back to Saxon House the Guv'nor treated us to cham-pagne."

It is right and fitting that Darkie Deacon should be almost as well known in the racing world as the jockeys who ride in public the horses he schools on the downs. His calm, nerve-less riding of The Dikler – which contributed so much to the horse's success – was greatly admired by the racing Press.

As a leading member of it, John Oaksey, said to me, "he just *is* a horseman, it's a sort of magic."

When Darkie Deacon led the new champion towards the winner's enclosure after the 1973 Cheltenham Gold Cup, someone among the hordes of cheering spectators shouted, "Well done Darkie;" and Fulke told him, "You know it's your day."

Chapter 7

THE DIKLER AS A STEEPLECHASER

"I think Willie Robinson must have been sad having to decide to retire just when another star was to appear at Saxon House," Peggy August reflected. "So with this in mind I consider that he rode The Dikler with great skill and patience. He taught him the basics of steeplechasing without any hope of reaping the benefits; yet without them my horse would have got even more headstrong and nothing would have been gained." And she agrees with Nick Gaselee that Willie made The Dikler look an easy ride.

The Dikler was first put to the test on the racecourse in the Honeybourne Novices' Chase at Cheltenham in November 1969. "The locals knew about him and some had seen him in point-to-points," said his owner. "There were several useful horses in this race, and it was hoped that mine would put up a good show. Willie tucked him in the middle of the field, but at the top of the hill on the last circuit it looked as though he had blown up; then, coming downhill, he overtook all the runners save two. But when they came to the last fence he crashed right through it, ending up literally on his nose. However, he recovered immediately to storm up the hill and win. I was beyond looking by then. Fulke said afterwards, 'He is very fast, and you will of course have a lot of buyers after him.' "

The racing Press were enthusiastic about the newcomer they were to hail as a successor to Mill House, and commented on his amazing acceleration in the final stages of the race. Indeed nothing could have been more impressive than the way The Dikler, having been almost on the floor at the fence which Stubbs II and Saccone had already taken in their stride, made his acrobatic recovery to pass this experienced pair going up the hill. It was one of the most remarkable performances put up by a novice at Cheltenham for some years.

But was The Dikler as good as he looked? Certain rival trainers believed that his win in the Honeybourne Chase was a fluke, and that he would not be able to clobber a fence like a runaway tank again and get away with it. Yet his next race, the Hopeful Novices' Chase at Newbury, he won in fine style, again ridden by Willie Robinson (who did not retire until the end of the 1970 season); in this he improved upon the promise he had displayed at Cheltenham, showing an ability to quicken which few horses of his size and strength possessed.

From the beginning, The Dikler could draw crowds. National Hunt enthusiasts had been waiting for a steeplechaser of note after the rather dreary period since the disappearance of Arkle from the scene through fracturing a pedal bone in his foot; and The Dikler's magnificant appearance made him the cynosure of all eyes at Newbury. Despite the unpromising weather, people deserted the stands and bars to watch him in the parade ring. John Lawrence (now Oaksey) wrote in the *Sunday Telegraph* that if he was offered a horse for Christmas he would like The Dikler, please, though Willie Robinson would have to help with his steering. It was also after the Hopeful Chase that the owner of another horse who had been placed in it said that he did not like The Dikler because he was like a giraffe; two months later, the same person asked a friend of Peggy's if she thought the horse could be bought, and named a large sum. The friend remarked "Oh, but that is a lot of money to give for a giraffe" – which effectively ended the conversation.

The bay gelding with the distinctive blaze and three white socks was the most discussed novice when he went to Warwick for his next race. Having missed two races owing to frost, he was badly in need of this one; but in the Crompton Chase he only got as far as the fourth fence, where he unseated his jockey when he stumbled on landing, took a stride and then slipped up. "Willie jumped back on him, and how he did it I shall never know," said Peggy.

"He is a small man and The Dikler is 17.2 h.h. They jumped the next fence before pulling up. The others were too far ahead by that time."

It was hoped that The Dikler would wipe out this disappointment when he ran in the Walter Hyde Handicap Chase at Kempton a fortnight later; and here he not only delighted his admirers, but gained many more when he pulverised the other top-class chasers in the race, never being headed after taking the lead at the thirteenth fence. Although carrying top weight, he flew over the remaining obstacles. Bannons Star, in receipt of a stone and tipped to beat him, could find no extra from two out; and Charter Flight, who had moved up threateningly four from home, was unable to quicken in the final stages. It was then that Willie Robinson came to the conclusion that The Dikler's stride was even longer than that of Mill House. "After this race," he said, "I felt 135 years old; but winning did the Guv'nor so much good that he looked half his age."

The Dikler's career during this time was full of ups and downs. But that dazzling performance at Kempton had proved that he was no nine-days wonder; so the spectators who flocked to Ascot for his appearance in the eagerly-awaited Grange Chase were shocked and frustrated when he overjumped at the second fence and came down. The Dikler and Irish Moss, a promising eight-year-old from Josh Gifford's stable, had been expected to provide one of the most exciting clashes of the season, and interest quickly evaporated when the former ended up on the floor and the latter was so exhausted by the heavy ground that he was pulled up before the second last. Another good novice, New Romney, ran out of steam after making the running for two miles.

The Dikler, affirmed one racing correspondent, may still be a great steeplechaser when he remains upright; and to prove that the horse was worthy of a place in the Cheltenham Gold Cup, Fulke Walwyn did not saddle him for Kempton's Galloway Braes Chase, in which he would have had only three opponents, but ran him instead against the tougher opposition in the Coventry Pattern Handicap Chase the same day. Since The Dikler was still a novice, Willie Robinson rode him with great restraint, keeping him at the back of the field for the first few fences. This race, in fact, was won virtually from pillar to post by the very useful Titus Oates, ridden with great tactical skill by Stan Mellor. The Dikler gave such a superb display of jumping, and produced such a burst of speed up the short run-in, that Titus Oates only just held on to win by a neck. To come second to a horse like this was very satisfactory, and The Dikler was now learning the virtues of calmness, and how to jump fences in public the way they should be jumped. All the same, John Lawrence could not resist writing that The Dikler had given his jockey his usual feel – which was roughly comparable with sitting on an active volcano.

Peggy August says she will never forget the thrill of that Cheltenham Gold Cup in 1970, "because in the parade before the race all the horses have a sheet with their name on it, and The Dikler had his for the first time. I thought, *this is the ultimate, he has really got there*. I did not mind whether he was in the money or not. I was so proud that he was in such good company."

Some doubt had been expressed in print as to whether The Dikler was ready for such a race, but his trainer reckoned that the horse would be better on wide left-hand turns at Cheltenham than he was on the tight right-hand track at Kempton. Two much-fancied runners were Spanish Steps and Kinloch Brae. The former had won his last three races and the latter his last four, and both had been beaten only once that season, on their first appearance. In the end, however, it was the American-owned Irish-trained L'Escargot, ridden by Tommy Carberry, who won the race. Kinloch Brae, who started favourite, fell in the lead at the 20th fence, and Spanish Steps finished third, behind another Irish-trained horse, French Tan.

The Dikler had been going well until he got to the hill on

the second circuit. Then he over-jumped and fell. It was the last time that he was to fall, but he had pulled a muscle off his stifle joint, and was to remain unsound until the middle of the summer.

Willie Robinson's retirement from race-riding was now imminent, and on the 18th April, a month after the Cheltenham Gold Cup was run, Peggy August and her husband received the following letter:–

> Tumbleweed Cottage,
> Lambourn,
> Berkshire
>
> Dear Mr. & Mrs. August,
>
> This is just a line to say that with much reluctance I have decided to retire from steeplechasing at the end of this season. I should like to take the opportunity of thanking you for all the kindness that you have shown me in the past year. Best wishes for every success with The Dikler in the future.
>
> Yours sincerely,
> William and Susan.

Soon after this, Willie Robinson went back to his native Ireland to start his own stable at The Curragh; and it was announced in the Press that Stan Mellor (though smaller and lighter than Willie) would ride Fulke Walwyn's young chaser next season.

The Dikler's numerous supporters now looked forward to seeing the new partnership in action, and they got their first sight of it in the Clanfield Handicap Chase at Newbury in November 1970. It had been in the Honeybourne Chase the previous season that Peggy had first seen her horse in a strange bit; she did not know what it was, and she did not like the look of it, and over the next few months she kept on suggesting to Fulke Walwyn that the puckle should be replaced by a grakle, a crossed noseband designed to keep a horse's head down and his mouth shut. Fulke, however, was adamant that no chaser like hers was raced in a grakle, and The Dikler had continued to wear his puckle for a season. Peggy now got her way, and the noseband (which is attached to hooks which fit under the bit and enables the rider to keep the bit up in the horse's mouth, thereby giving him much more control) was taken off for the race at Newbury.

The Dikler started a heavily-backed favourite, only to throw away his chances by his exaggerated jumping to the left. Although he was giving Sweet Score 27 lbs., he had the race at his mercy and could have come home alone. He was leading by twelve lengths when he approached the fourth from home and ran right down the fence, thus allowing Sweet Score to greatly reduce his lead. He could still have won if only he had jumped straight at the last fence, but once more he went violently to the left; and though he fought back up the run-in, he failed to catch Sweet Score, a horse trained by Fred Winter and ridden by Paul Kelleway, and went under by threequarters of a length.

Peggy blames herself for what happened in this race, and her horse was never raced again without wearing a puckle. "Stan rang me up that evening and begged me to let the puckle go back on him," she says. "He told me that if I didn't the horse would kill himself; and he also said that being run away with twice in one race had never happened to him before!"

A horse who steers like a car on black ice would have to mend his ways and not repeat such regrettable behaviour if he wished to be taken seriously as a future champion, warned one racing correspondent. The Dikler must have taken note of this, because he won his next race, the Tony Teacher Handicap Chase at Cheltenham in December, when Barry Brogan rode him, by fifteen lengths. He is a cracker when he jumps like this, noted Britain's leading racing paper, *The Sporting Life*; and Peggy August received a case of whisky from the family of the course official after whom the race is named.

The Dikler was now being described as the most exciting horse in racing, and it was clear that he had to be built up for another crack at the Cheltenham Gold Cup. Past errors, however, made him far from a safe proposition, and one paper went so far as to call him the most difficult horse in Europe to ride; but his fan club was increasing all the time, and he had well and truly caught the imagination of the public, besides proving a wonderful source of copy for the Press.

The 1970 King George VI Chase at Kempton on Boxing Day had been snowed off, and Stratford racegoers were looking forward to the unexpected pleasure of seeing The Dikler in action on December 30. He was naturally the star attraction, and attendance was up by two thirds on the previous year. So it was hardly surprising that a large section of the crowd erupted in anger when, after the horse had been declared for the Dark Strangers' Chase, Fulke Walwyn decided to withdraw him. He did so because he considered that two rebuilt fences on the course were too stiff for a young horse still being educated; both Stan Mellor and Barry Brogan, who rode in the first race, had warned him of the danger of the third and seventh fences. "It's as though it's got bloody trees growing in it," growled the trainer when commenting upon the latter fence, for which thicker birch had been used than for any of the others on the track.

"Those fences were very upright and starey when we went to look at them," recalls Peggy. "New brush had been cut; and with the sun on it, it looked dazzlingly white. There were also some very thick pieces. Fulke thought that as my horse was still a novice it would not be wise to risk him in these conditions. I was of the same opinion myself. Those fences were not even uniform, nor had they been inspected by the Clerk of the Course. If the Stewards decide that your reason for withdrawing is justifiable, you are permitted to withdraw. But in this case they took the opposite view and we were fined £25.

The Dikler's next race was the 2-mile Hungerford Chase at Newbury in January, and it did seem then as if he had learnt something from the mistakes he had made on his last visit to Newbury, for his mighty leaps could not have been straighter. Sonny Somers was not an opponent to be taken lightly, but he was unable to match strides with The Dikler, who did not go until Stan Mellor let him, jumping to the front after the third last and winning easily. He had been, in his jockey's words, "just like a big Teddy Bear, kind, amiable and lovely to play with," giving him a ride beyond his wildest dreams. Fulke, too, was delighted with his Cheltenham hope, who had done all that was expected of him and more.

But after demolishing Sonny Somers again a week later in the Thunder and Lightning Chase at Ascot, where he gave an exhibition performance and galloped his solitary opponent into the ground, he had one of those inexplicable lapses which the people involved in his career found so baffling. The Gainsborough Chase at Sandown was a crucial examination for him to pass, since he was receiving 9 lbs. from French Tan and a stone from Titus Oates. Willie Robinson had considered French Tan, the runner-up to L'Escargot in the 1970 Cheltenham Gold Cup, the finest staying steeplechaser in Ireland; but it was jumping errors that relegated The Dikler to third place, combined with an unexpected lack of co-operation. He had been second to Titus Oates for most of the race, but then hit the eleventh fence and pecked on landing over the thirteenth. Though The Dikler continued to press Titus Oates, French Tan, who had been well behind the two leaders at one point, ran on to such effect that he got up to beat the Saxon House representative by half a length for second place.

As Stan pointed out, The Dikler had been treated kindly by the handicappers and should have won. "Instead, when it came to the crunch on that day, he did not want to accelerate, but tended to hang behind the other two when I asked him to go on and win." This performance was a big disappointment to his jockey, who formed the opinion that he was a sulky character, and said so to the equally disappointed Fulke Walwyn. "I admit," says Stan, that I was wrong in my judgment." But it seemed to be confirmed when, in his last race before the National Hunt Festival, The Dikler returned to his erratic ways.

The opposition in the Manifesto Handicap Chase at Lingfield was weak. Nevertheless, The Dikler settled quite well, and Stan found that holding him that afternoon was not really difficult. "Only, being such a good jumper, he kept jumping up to the front, and at an open ditch he again jumped there. After the Sandown experience, I decided that I would not try to pull him around; but I should have kept him behind another horse until he had passed the sharp bend beyond the stands, because what happened was that he veered sharply out to the right. We didn't make it and ended up heading towards the wood. We lost many lengths, but even this handicap shouldn't have been enough for him to get beaten by Arctic Actress."

"Yes," said Peggy, "he almost disappeared into the silver birches, and you could see it was going to happen after he had jumped himself into the lead, because when he went past the stands he had his neck stretched out and this spelt disaster, as there was no way that any jockey could gain control. All the way down to Lingfield the conversation had been gay and lively in the car, as we had with us one of the Cheltenham stewards, Colonel John Chamberlayne, the owner of Marksman, who was to finish third in the race, and the retired whipper-in of the Heythrop, Percy Durno. When I got back to the car feeling rather despondent, Percy said to me, 'Oh but Ma'am, wouldn't he go down the Clapton Vale well!' – Clapton Vale being prime hunting country."

It is interesting to hear what Stan Mellor has to say about

The Dikler. When I talked to the man who was champion jockey three times and now trains successfully at Lambourn, he was big enough to say frankly that he was not the right jockey for the horse. Yet while The Dikler was certainly not among his favourite chasers, he still maintained that he was the best jumper in England. "I always said, 'put him in the National and he'll win it.' But it was too late when he did get to Aintree. He had a one-track mind in those days. He only wanted to go, and could be very difficult to settle. What he always needed in a race was a pacemaker." Stan then went on to tell me what a safe and comfortable jumper The Dikler was. "He was precise at his fences, and his landing gear was so excellent that it felt as though you were landing on cushions."

Both Peggy August and Fulke Walwyn had wanted Stan to ride The Dikler, and Stan could not see the point of trying to hold the horse up. "I thought," he said, "that it was better to let him go and get on with it. Well, as you know, it didn't work out too well in our first race together at Newbury. And when I was prevented by injury from riding him in his next race, the Tony Teacher at Cheltenham, and Barry Brogan took my place, he held him up and won on him. This was what made me reverse my tactics on our second appearance at Newbury. But after The Dikler had run out with me at Lingfield it was said that I couldn't ride him; and it is true that, in a way, he was a disaster for me. He was a big jockey's horse. Terry Biddlecombe would have been ideal."

Stan thinks that perhaps he was unfortunate in riding The Dikler when he did. "He had had one or two falls with Willie Robinson through overjumping and Mr. Walwyn thought that to get his confidence back it would be best to run him in small races. But, in fact, those in which the gallops were slow made him a far more difficult horse to handle, as I found out the hard way. On the gallops he would pull and pull and pull and I always said Darkie Deacon deserved medals for riding him some mornings."

So had Stan found him difficult to hold in races? "Yes, but not at a fast gallop. When he got going he had a very strong gallop and his stride was tremendous, besides which he was a stayer. Then, later on, Mr. Walwyn asked me if I would mind if Barry Brogan rode him the next season. He thought that I had lost faith in the horse."

Darkie Deacon has a lot of sympathy for Stan Mellor. He says: "The year Stan was engaged to ride The Dikler he was badly injured, so he never really got to know him – which meant that it was like trying to do the impossible, for The Dikler was definitely a horse who needed a lot of understanding."

Meeting Stan, it is difficult to realise that he once needed plastic surgery after both jaw and cheek bone were smashed in the first running of the Schweppes Gold Trophy when he was thrown and practically the whole field galloped over him. At another meeting, he was in agonising pain after a fall when two horses galloped over him. Yet he made so little of it that he not only rode in the next race but won it. It is not surprising to learn that, though such experiences had no effect upon Stan's nerve, he has done a great deal to encourage new safety devices for jump jockeys through the National Hunt Jockeys' Association formed in 1964 and now amalgamated with its flat-race counterpart. Stan Mellor possesses a deep feeling for horses and hated using the whip during his racing career. Instead he concentrated on riding them with hands and heels, telling inexperienced jockeys whom he thinks use the whip too much to try a little tenderness instead.

Yet another injury prevented Stan Mellor from riding The Dikler in the 1971 Cheltenham Gold Cup, and so Barry Brogan had the ride. The question now was, would The Dikler take command and go his own way, which, when he was in his express-train mood, meant trouble, or would he show that he really was becoming a reformed character? Despite the way he had been humbled at Lingfield by Arctic Actress, he was backed down from 9-1 to 15-2.

The going was heavy, but the reigning champion, L'Escargot, who had returned from a trip to the United States to defend his title, was still able to draw away from Leap Frog on the run-in to win for the second year in succession. The Dikler, who had pulled hard in the early stages of the race, finished a well-beaten third. But he had run his best race of the season and could not be disregarded as a possible winner here in the future. But was he, one racing correspondent wondered, too strong for Stan Mellor? Had this brilliant jockey the physical strength to check such massive power when the occasion demanded it, or should the horse always be ridden by someone built on the lines of Barry Brogan?

Fulke Walwyn wrote to tell Peggy August that he was satisfied with her horse's running in the Gold Cup, and that the combination of the horrible underfoot conditions and the ridiculous pace at which the race was run had worn him down. The Dikler, he said, was a very tired horse the next day, but had picked up quicker than he had expected him to and was eating up well. "Let's give him another week before we decide whether to run or not," he wrote. "I have a very soft spot for the big horse, and though he gives us some shocks he also gives me some great thrills. I feel next spring that we should concentrate on two or three-and-a-half miles to start with, as they will be better-contested races and not so tiring for him. There is no doubt that he is a very fast horse, with perhaps stamina doubts. These thoughts do not mean that I want to rule out the Gold Cup but I would rather wait and see plans. I enclose the photo I love which I meant to give you ages ago winning at Newbury."

Commenting on what Fulke had written, Peggy said, "This shows his concern for the horse and how he likes to discuss vague possible future plans with the owner, and it confirms that The Dikler had speed – which is contrary to that public opinion which thought he was just a slogger."

The Dikler's fame had now spread abroad, and the

Americans were keen to see such a bold, fearless jumper in their country. So he was one of the three horses from England invited to take part in the 1971 Colonial Cup run over 2 miles 6½ furlongs at Camden in South Carolina. It was a great compliment, and the Colonial Cup Committee would have paid the cost of transport as well as that of his owner, trainer and jockey both ways. "But we had to refuse," said Peggy, "though I would love to have gone if we had not had to consider the horse. He had been raced until March, and to get him fit to race in October would have meant getting him up months beforehand. So he would have had hardly any rest at all – he was a horse who needed a lot of road work."

Instead of crossing the Atlantic, Fulke Walwyn decided to let The Dikler take his chance in the Mackeson Gold Cup at Cheltenham, having been pleased with the way the horse had run in the Top Rank Chase at Ascot on his first appearance of the new season when he came second to Crisp. At Cheltenham, in a field of seasoned chasers, The Dikler was the best handicapped horse, with only 11 st. 2 lbs. to carry, and he was receiving weight from horses he had beaten. Under Barry Brogan's careful tuition, The Dikler ran as straight as a gun barrel. But when Royal Relief was brought down when Kippie Lodge lurched into him at the eighth, he cannoned into The Dikler and caught him on the flanks with his hind legs, leaving two clear hoof prints. Given time to recover by Barry, The Dikler still managed to finish fourth to Gay Trip. This race gave Peggy real encouragement, and she said she really enjoyed watching it, adding that her horse "always slowed up at Cheltenham coming down the hill – he never seemed to find his stride there, and, having such a big one, the ground was always falling away from him. So he had a lot of ground to make up at the end, but was closing the gap."

In December, The Dikler was at Cheltenham again for the Massey Ferguson Gold Cup, and his owner went home from Prestbury Park further encouraged by his placing; in a tremendous finish Leap Frog only just held him off by a head, and he would have won in another few strides. Behind him in third place was Titus Oates, and further behind still was Gay Trip. Top weight in this race was carried by Crisp, the beloved Australian horse whose astonishing performance in the 1973 Grand National, when it was only in the last few yards that he was caught by Red Rum, will never be forgotten by those who saw it. Despite his big weight, Crisp made most of the running until he ruined his chances with a mistake at the last open ditch.

Leap Frog's win was a particularly popular one, because he was trained by Tom Dreaper, who was making a final trip to Cheltenham before handing over the Kilsallaghan Stables to his son; and the old man, whose name will always be associated with Arkle, received a great ovation.

The Dikler was a controversial steeplechaser who had been overpraised and then reviled, wrote a racing journalist, and certainly there had been occasions in the past when his tearaway tactics had proved his downfall, because a horse who fights for his head uses up the energy that is needed at the end of a race in order to win it. It seemed that until The Dikler learned not to squander stamina and waste strength he had little hope of landing the top prizes. But Fulke Walwyn's faith in this son of Vulgan never faltered, and on the 27th December, 1971, his charge reached the heights that he had so often promised to scale. This was the day The Dikler won his first classic, the King George VI Chase at Kempton, where the strong opposition included such well-known names as Spanish Steps, L'Escargot, The Laird, Titus Oates (whose trainer, Gordon W. Richards, thought he would take a lot of beating) and Glencaraig Lady, who had won the Irish Grand National and started favourite.

The Dikler was helped by a strong front-runner in the shape of Titus Oates. So he didn't have to be held up at any fence – if this happened when he wanted to go faster, he either boiled over or lost concentration. Jumping freely, without a single wayward thought in his head, he won by half a length from Spanish Steps before a record crowd; and as she patted him in the unsaddling enclosure, his delighted owner said aloud, "There now, you've made it and proved that you are a good horse." And a woman from South Oxfordshire who heard her say it, said, "We've always known he was." "So," says Peggy, "I came home very elated in spite of the trials of the day." And there were trials, for the owners' car park had been full when she got to the meeting and she had to leave her car in the road; there were no racecards left; she was told that the last sandwich had been eaten, and that the whisky had run out in the bar.

In January 1972 Darkie Deacon received a cheque with this letter from Signett Farm, a letter he has treasured, together with others that Peggy August wrote him during the time that her horse was in his care:—

> Dear Darkie,
>
> Time flies but I meant to write to you a fortnight ago after Tuppenny's very fine win in the King George. I really could hardly believe that at last he'd made his big win – not that he did not deserve it the way he has been going this season, but because at times I feel that he is not the luckiest of horses. I am glad to see the Press have given credit to you – fancy having headlines in the *Sunday Telegraph*, I hope you felt justly proud. Mrs. Walwyn says you've had your tankard* engraved. With best wishes to you and your horses for 1972,
>
> Peggy August.

* Darkie had been presented with this tankard when The Dikler was adjudged the best turned-out horse at Ascot on the day he finished second to Crisp in the Top Rank Club Chase there.

The Dikler had clearly found the right jockey in Barry Brogan, whose handling of the horse was widely praised. Maybe he isn't the most stylish of jockeys. But The Dikler did not want a stylist; he wanted a good strong jockey, which Barry was.

For his second Thunder and Lightning Chase at Ascot, The Dikler went down to the start like a dose of salts. But once the race was on, he settled well and proceeded to give his rivals a lesson in how to jump, winning in a canter. It was that afternoon that Peggy August appeared on television, because Fulke had said she would without her knowledge. "I was very nervous as I never wanted to be in the limelight. I remember that the first thing the interviewer said to me was, 'You are famous for your hats,' and I told him that I only wore them when I went racing."

The following month, The Dikler returned to Kempton to run in the Coventry Pattern Chase. Crisp was tipped to beat both The Dikler and Titus Oates, and duly did so, giving weight away all round. Barry Brogan had counted on a fast pace only to find that this time Titus Oates was a reluctant leader; so as the pace was not fast enough for The Dikler, he wasn't able to relax. In fact, he had quite a battle with the horse to prevent him from hitting the front too soon; but he had to let him go on after the twelfth fence, and at the final bend Crisp moved up, took the lead over the last and went on to win by $2\frac{1}{2}$ lengths.

These two great horses met again in the 1972 Cheltenham Gold Cup; and here, on sticky ground, Crisp was to fail for lack of stamina and The Dikler come third, as he had done the year before. Again he had gone to the front too soon, and although he led over the last fence he was caught in the run-in and beaten threequarters of a length and a head by the Irish mare Glencaraig Lady and Royal Toss. The dual Gold Cup winner L'Escargot, who had looked a distinct danger three fences out, finished fourth, seven lengths behind The Dikler. Titus Oates never showed with a chance. Glencaraig Lady, a faller in the 1971 race, thus became the second mare to win the Gold Cup (the first was Kerstin in 1958).

As The Dikler was not too tired after this effort, it was decided to take him over to Ireland for the Irish Grand National at Fairyhouse 18 days later. "But there seemed to be a jinx on it from the beginning," recalls Peggy. "Fulke flew over early and I went on the Monday. The Dikler was also flying, but instead of arriving in the morning he did not touch down until the late afternoon because after he had been loaded a newspaper van backed into his aeroplane and damaged it, so he had to wait for a replacement. This upset Fulke, who was extremely tired after waiting about all day; and we also knew that the course was too wet for our horse, since it was literally a quagmire. There was very nearly water standing on it. However, if we hadn't run him we would have forfeited our travelling allowance."

The ordeal took so much out of The Dikler that he was pulled up half-way round the course. The Irish Grand National fences are not at all like those at Aintree. They look more like those built for a point-to-point; and the race was won by an Irish horse named Dim Wit more accustomed to such soggy ground in a country which has one of the heaviest rainfalls in Western Europe.

That race was The Dikler's last of the 1971/72 season. His first race of the 1972/73 season was the Massey Ferguson Gold Cup at Cheltenham in December, when he was set to carry the top weight of 12 st. 3 lbs. A superlative jump landed him ahead of Arctic Bow three fences out, but he was unable to maintain the advantage. The attempt to give away more than a stone all round told so much on him in the last half mile that Soloning deprived him of second place. The winner, Arctic Bow, was magnificently ridden by Andy Turnell. But at least one journalist thought that it was The Dikler who took the chief honours.

The King George VI Chase, The Dikler's next race, was introduced when the Kempton Park executive thought that there should be a good weight for age steeplechase over the

Christmas holiday to bring out the best staying steeple-chasers. Many people regard this race as a stepping stone on the way to the Cheltenham Gold Cup. The fences are stiff and the course, being triangular, with tight right-hand turns, favours nippy little horses. So The Dikler, with his enormous stride, was not really suited even though he came to Kempton with a success in the race under his belt. This time it was won by Pendil, running in his first three-mile steeplechase. The Dikler followed him home; and it is interesting to note that Dim Wit, who had come over from Ireland for it, finished fourth.

The Dikler, however, was to have a satisfactory Gold Cup trial in his next race at Wincanton, over a course well suited to long-striding chasers. Here, in the John Bull Chase, run over 2 miles 5 furlongs, he started favourite and won unchallenged from I'm Happy. The Laird, who started third favourite, led to the eleventh and then dropped out quickly. Royal Toss, the second favourite, would have pre-ferred softer going and proved no threat.

Returning to Wincanton a fortnight later, and running over the same distance, The Dikler had no difficulty dispos-ing of I'm Happy in a two-horse race. "People said he had only a novice to beat," said Peggy, "but my horse was never off the bit and won in a canter." One who took a rather different view of things was Richard Pitman, who was due to ride Pendil in the Cheltenham Gold Cup and was more confident than ever of his horse's chance. He told reporters, "There is nothing here that impresses me." (When Peggy saw Fulke Walwyn the following week, Fulke said to her, "He'll regret those words.")

Three weeks later The Dikler made his last appearance before the Gold Cup. It was over a figure-of-eight course at Windsor, and he didn't care for it at all. One of two courses in the country which is bounded by the Thames and a millstream, Windsor has horses on some sort of bend most of the time. It was obvious to Peggy August that such a course was going to be a difficult one for "Tuppeny," and already the day had started badly, as that morning Barry Brogan had been fined for doing a U turn on a motorway and Fulke was not well and could not go to the meeting.

The Dikler, opposed by Spanish Steps and the moderate Fortune Bay II, negotiated the corners all right, but after jumping the last fence in front he hung badly to the left and was relegated to second place by the Stewards for taking Spanish Steps' ground. "He went right across my horse," said the latter's courageous owner, Edward Courage, who is confined to a wheelchair. But a friend Peggy had taken with her to Windsor consoled her by telling her that a bad rehearsal meant a good performance next time. "We brought Barry back with us to Burford," said Peggy, "as he was banned from driving, and somehow I took the wrong route on the M4 and we found ourselves going towards London; and Barry said cheerfully, 'Oh never mind, just do a U turn.' "

The scribes who had been so lavish in their praise when The Dikler had won the King George VI Chase in 1971 were now busy censuring him for his behaviour in the Fairlawne Chase at Windsor, one of them referring to him as this extraordinary animal who went up the straight like a drunken crab; while another told his readers that if The Dikler had been allowed to go on long enough he would have taken Spanish Steps with him into the river.

That ride at Windsor was to be Barry Brogan's last on the horse he had done so much to make. Plagued by ill health, he was unable to avert a breakdown and, at the age of 26, he returned to Ireland. "He was," says Peggy, "a fearless horseman on a fearless horse, and it was a breathtaking sight to see them jumping, especially over the schooling fences which The Dikler took flat out. Barry was explicit; he always gave me a very good account of each race, and he had great charm. He rode my horse as well as anyone could at that period of his career; and if he was perhaps a bit impetuous in that he anticipated victories which didn't always come, he was undoubtedly a very good jockey."

Pendil leading The Dikler (left) over the last fence in the 1973

Chapter 8

THE DIKLER'S GOLD CUP

TALKING to me about the 1973 Cheltenham Gold Cup, Peggy August said, "I never really expected my horse to win it, there were so many good horses in the race that season – Pendil, Charlie Potheen, Spanish Steps and L'Escargot among them; and the previous year he was in front too soon – he likes something to chase."

Some months before the race was due to be run, and realising that Charlie Potheen and The Dikler, the two stable companions, would both be running in it, Peggy was certain that Barry Brogan, who, as first jockey to Fulke Walwyn, would have had the choice of mount, would choose Charlie Potheen. So she had said to her trainer, "What about engaging another jockey for The Dikler?" She had in mind Terry Biddlecombe, but Fulke only replied that it was a long way off and that it was best to "leave things."

As it turned out, Barry Brogan did decide to ride The Dikler, and Terry Biddlecombe was engaged to ride Charlie Potheen. "Then," says Peggy, "when Barry was taken ill and had to go into a Dublin nursing home, we asked Terry whom he would recommend to take his place. Fortunately, he suggested Ron Barry. None of us had met Ron at the time, as he did most of his racing in the North. The day before he was going to school The Dikler, he was taking part in the Jockeys' Show Jumping Championship at the National Equestrian Centre at Stoneleigh in Warwickshire. I was to meet him at Saxon House, and when I got there Fulke said to me, 'Did you see Stoneleigh on television last night?' And when I said that I had, he said, 'What a disaster Ron Barry was. I have my doubts.' "

Just at the time this conversation was taking place, Ron Barry turned up and they set off for the downs. The Dikler went flat out with Ron over three fences, and Fulke Walwyn's comment on this performance was, "Well thank God he is a better jockey than he is a show jumper!"

Peggy August went to Cheltenham with her husband, David, and two friends. She thought then that The Dikler's prospects would be improved by the presence in the field of Charlie Potheen to provide a fast pace, which, as a strong front-runner he could undoubtedly do. "Actually," she said, "I could see Charlie winning; but then all the horses were dangerous to me. As expected, Charlie set off at a furious gallop and Pendil was also going very well. On the first circuit The Dikler was near the rear of the field. On the second, Charlie at last began to tire, and Ron wanted my horse to go on the inside so that he would have the advantage of the running rail. In fact, he had to go on the outside. Then, on the long run up the hill, he snaked back on the inside. I was watching from the green, and as The Dikler went by me up the straight he was several lengths behind Pendil. I did not believe that he could catch him – Pendil had great finishing speed. But people were beginning to shout The Dikler's name and I knew by then that he would be placed. So I began to make my way to the unsaddling enclosure, to be met by Cath Walwyn in tears. For a moment I thought that something terrible had happened to the old horse; then I realised that they were tears of joy because he had won. Fulke was gesticulating – which he does when he is very excited – and it was Darkie Deacon who led The Dikler into the unsaddling enclosure, because I don't think it is fair to let the boys who have done all the hard work be deprived of this honour."

It was certainly a dramatic finish, and the spectators were thrilled by it. Pendil, who had won his last eleven races, was beaten by a short head, and Charlie Potheen finished third, in front of L'Escargot. Pendil's trainer, who lives next door to the Walwyns at Lambourn and is a friend of theirs, was the first to offer his congratulations. The Queen Mother, looking very charming in a blue coat and hat, invited Peggy to tea in her box, after she had presented her with the Cup. "She was very easy to talk to and asked me where I lived. Then our conversation was chiefly about horses."

Peggy admits that she had hardly come down to earth when it was time to go home; and then, when she arrived in the car park, she realised that she had lost the Cup. "I had put it down somewhere and just left it there, because when David Nicholson, the trainer, came up and said, 'Let's look at it,' I simply could not remember where I had put it. We ran back to the stands and asked the security police to help me find it; and eventually the Secretary heard that the jeweller had taken it back to his shop in the town where it had come from. By then the shop was closed, so she kindly rang up the owner at his home, and he came out and opened up the shop so that I could take the Cup home with me. That night I went to the Lamb Inn in Burford to cele-brate with my family and friends." A few days later she wrote Darkie Deacon the following letter:–

Signett Farm,
Burford,
Oxon.

Dear Darkie,

It is with great pleasure that I send you the enclosed present from the Gold Cup. This is the big win we've always hoped The Dikler capable of. I know that it has been a long time to come and we have had to suffer some ups and downs to get it, but the style he did it in was great.

I hear the photography session went off very well. I can imagine how nice he will look – rather proud – he knows so well when he is the centre of attraction. Thank you again for all the care you have given my horse, it is not for nothing that the Press

have linked your name with his. I am glad to
see that even Audax gave 'Tuppeny' some
praise in last week's *Horse and Hound*. Have a
good summer and I look forward to seeing
you again next season.

Yours sincerely,
Peggy August.

And she was sent this letter by her happy trainer:–

Saxon House,
Lambourn,
Berks.

My dear Peggy,

Thank you so much for your very generous present to the lads. They appreciate it so
much. They're a good lot and when something like this happens it's grand to be able
to give them something extra. It was wonderful, wasn't it? I felt so proud of The Dikler
for the way that he produced that speed and
unbeatable determination. I hope you saw
the re-run on Sports View last night. It really
shows how unlucky we would have been if
we'd been beaten. Ron said at the time that if
he hadn't tried to go the wrong side of Charlie at the second last he would have only
been a length behind Pendil at the last, in
fact where we wanted him to be. What a
jump he made at that last fence, he must
have gained a length in the air. He's just
gone prancing out of the yard in great form
and ready for his hols again. My sincere
thanks for your present for the lads. I am so
thrilled that The Dik has really done his stuff

and that you should own a Gold Cup winner."

Peggy's comment on this letter was, "I think it shows his
feeling towards the horse, lads and owner, and it is worth
noting that there is no mention of his own skills."

To many it had seemed before the 1973 Gold Cup that
Richard Pitman and Pendil presented such an invincible
combination that it was inconceivable that a twelfth victory
would not be achieved at Cheltenham; and The Dikler's
antics at Windsor had not, of course, done anything to
advertise his reputation for reliability. It was even said by
one critic that he was not in the same class as Fred Winter's
horse; and in fact he started third favourite at 9-1, with
Pendil at 4-6 and Charlie Potheen at 9-2.

Ron Barry was never a jockey to be overawed by reputations, and when he met The Dikler an alliance was formed
between two strong and fearless characters who brought
out the best qualities in each other. Twice champion jockey,
this tall Irishman was born in Limerick, where his father
had a small farm and greengrocer's. He comes from a large
Catholic family, and ever since he could walk he enjoyed
trying out the ponies on the farm. In his own words, "If a
loaf of bread was wanted from the village I rode on a pony,
never a bicycle, to fetch it." Asked if he did well at school,
he answered that he did not go very often, and added, "I
was away hunting or at point-to-points; and one day I had
set off to go there when I remembered that there was a local
race meeting. So I dropped my satchel of books over the
church wall, where it was found by the priest, who took it
to the headmaster. I got into terrible trouble." The headmaster had had Ron and his parents up before him many
times before. "He wanted to chuck me out," said Ron. Yet
strangely enough the future champion never failed in the
exams which were held at the end of the term. "I always
managed to scrape through," he said. Perhaps, though,
one should feel some sympathy for that headmaster.

Darkie Deacon leading in The Dikler after his victory in the 1973 Cheltenham Gold Cup. Fulke Walwyn, The Dikler's trainer, is on the right.

At fourteen, Ron weighed only six and a half stone, and he was small. "I did not grow to my present height until I was nineteen, and by then I weighed ten and a half stone." In those days, Liam Ward was the champion jockey in Ireland, and Ron's parents arranged to meet him because they were keen for this son of theirs to ride on the Flat – at that time he had no interest in jumping. He started off in a humble way when, after his sixteenth birthday, he was apprenticed to a private trainer, Tommy Shaw. For the first six months he crushed oats or swept the yard and was not allowed to ride. "I could ride, but not as well as I thought I could, and I was still very small." Half-a-crown pocket money a week was all he received for his labour during the first two years. But he does not regret the time he spent in that yard, because he was able to go over to England with the travelling lad for three weeks on end and have fun there. "Whenever someone told me to make a wish I would wish to be a champion jockey like Liam."

Many boys who start off intending to make flat-racing their career find they become too heavy for it, and Ron Barry was one of them. Which was how he came to leave the horses belonging to Mrs. Anne Biddle and answered an advertisement for a job as box driver and jump jockey to Commander Campbell, who lived in Scotland. Although he had not got a driver's licence when he wrote off, he says he soon got one, and during that first year he rode five winners for the Commander. From then on success snowballed. "The jockey I admired so much in steeplechasing, Gerry Scott, used to give me a lot of good advice, and he would look after me in some of my early races. For example, he would make certain that my girths were tight enough, and when we jumped off he used to say, 'Follow me,' so as to get me in the best position early on."

In the early 'sixties Ron rode for Gordon W. Richards, who trains near Penrith; and it was while he was with the Penrith trainer that he won the title of Champion Jockey twice and also broke the record for the number of winners ridden in a single season. Modestly, he attributes his success to 60% luck and 40% skill. "After about ten years," he says, "we decided to go our own ways, though Mr. Richards had often let me off if I was offered good rides elsewhere."

Ron was freelancing when Terry Biddlecombe, one of the most popular and courageous jockeys of the decade, rang him to say that he had just put him up to ride The Dikler at Cheltenham in March, as Barry Brogan was unwell and he himself would be riding Charlie Potheen. As can readily be imagined, Ron was thrilled at the prospect of riding a horse like this in such a race as the Gold Cup. Ten days after his conversation with Terry Biddlecombe, Fulke Walwyn rang him up and asked him to go down to Lambourn to sit on The Dikler and give him a jump. "On my way south," says Ron, "I went show jumping at Stoneleigh, and Pat Buckley and I had a bet on how fast we could go round the course regardless of the number of jumps we knocked down. I rode shorter than usual, scattering poles; and Mr. Walwyn, who had been watching us on his television screen, rang up Terry and said, 'Good God, what a something something jockey you seem to have got me for tomorrow!"

Ron stayed that night with Richard Pitman, who at that time was first jockey to Fred Winter. "He drove me over to Saxon House, where I was introduced to Mr. Walwyn and The Dikler's owner, Mrs. Peggy August, who had arrived from Burford. But the exhaust of the Land Rover was broken and this made conversation difficult on our way to the jumps. When Mr. Walwyn did catch what I said I think he found it difficult to translate into English because of my brogue and the fact that I have lived in Scotland and Cumberland and do speak very fast and low."

Ron Barry's first impression of the horse with whom he was to realise his greatest ambition was that he was "an enormous, powerful beast." He discovered the horse's power as soon as he got up on him and The Dikler proceeded to fly over the fences at a breathtaking speed.

"Then," said Ron, "he pulled himself up. It was as if he knew exactly what he had to do. I was not on him long enough to find out anything more about him."

Fulke Walwyn told Ron that if the Gold Cup was run as he thought it would be, Charlie Potheen and Clever Scot would be the front-runners. "I reckoned that I would be able to handle The Dikler all right. What I did like when I came to ride him in races was that there was plenty in front of me and that I was comfortable on him straightaway; and from the first Darkie Deacon told me that I was on a Gold Cup winner. No, he didn't pull, he just took hold, and I never tried to teach him anything on the course because he knew more about it than I did."

After his trial with The Dikler at Saxon House, Ron returned to the North and continued racing, only to break his collarbone at Chepstow, an injury which he said nothing about in public since he was determined that it was not going to prevent him from riding in the Gold Cup. He stayed at Cheltenham the night before the race was run; and although Pendil was such a red-hot favourite he was not worried about the race itself. What he was desperately worried about was getting The Dikler down to the start without him running away. "Yes," says his pretty, fair-haired wife, Liz, who was then his fiancée, "whenever we met he would talk about it to me and he had that fear on his mind so much that I don't believe he thought of much else."

Fulke Walwyn, discussing the race with Ron in the paddock beforehand, warned him that the horse would take a breather half-way through it, and he was not to mind if he went badly for half a furlong, as The Dikler would drop the bit. "He told me," said Ron, "not to hit the front too soon; and then said that, if I could, to be fairly handy at the second last fence, and after that to make the best of my way home."

Ron Barry did not want more time to get to know his mount because it might have added to his anxiety. The prospect of such a strong horse running away to the start, as well as in the race, continued to haunt him, for he knew that with a broken collarbone he would be powerless to prevent this. The Dikler, however, did not misbehave on the way to the start; and once they were away Ron dropped his hands on his neck and rode him on a long rein. While The Dikler may have had an inclination to run away to the first fence, he soon realised that his new jockey was not going to pull on him; and after jumping it, "he seemed to go half asleep and so I had a dream of a ride," said Ron. "For once I had made no plans as to where I should try to place my horse. The race was being run at a good gallop and we were near the rear of the field. As The Dikler was jumping beautifully, it was almost like a good day's hunting; and in fact he felt like a very good hunter. But then, about a mile and a quarter from home, he suddenly went badly and I got extremely worried for a few strides before I realised that he was only having his breather, as Mr. Walwyn had said he would. Up till then I had been talking to him, urging him on, as he was so relaxed. When he suddenly switched into a different gear at the top of the hill, I knew that I was on a very fast horse."

Jumping the third last, Ron realised that he had a very good chance of winning. "Yet I still did not ask him to go all out. I tried to go on the inside of Charlie Potheen, who by now was tiring; and Terry, through no fault of his own, found his horse hanging towards the rails. So I switched to the outside. I had no idea how well Pendil was still going, but The Dikler jumped the second last magnificently, though that jump is not as big as the last. Between those two fences he had torn past Charlie and now he was really travelling," continued Ron. "The excitement was so great that I never felt my shoulder at all."

Half-way up the run-in Pendil seemed to wander off a straight line; and The Dikler, who was still full of running, won in a time of 6 minutes 37.2 seconds, the fastest time since Knock Hard's 6 minutes 28.4 seconds in 1953, and more than 20 seconds faster than the time Midnight Court took to win in 1979. Ron remembers how, as they pulled up, Dick Pitman said, 'Well done.' He remembers, too, the cheers as they entered the unsaddling enclosure, and how much The Queen Mother knew about The Dikler, because it surprised him. "When she congratulated me, I was so carried away by emotion that I hardly remember anything else. It is every jockey's aim to win the Cheltenham Gold Cup or the Grand National and it was not until the next day that I realised fully that I had won."

Among the tributes paid to Peggy August's horse after his sensational victory in the Cheltenham Gold Cup of 1973 was one from Michael Williams, who wrote in the monthly magazine, *Light Horse*, of which he is the Editor: "The Dikler's triumph will have delighted point-to-point enthusiasts, perhaps even those who have persistently decried him, a procedure which commenced before he even saw a course. 'What on earth makes you place a horse like that at the top of the line?' remarked a well-known horsedealer and judge when John Webber awarded The Dikler first prize in a class for novice hunters at the Thame Show."

The same writer then went on to ask whether Pendil was unlucky, and answered: "His jockey thought so, and blamed himself for the defeat. But after seeing the way The Dikler ate up the ground coming up the hill to the finish, no one is going to convince me that the horse who takes his name from a stream near Northleach does not deserve to go down in the history books along with such illustrious names as Golden Miller, Cottage Rake and Arkle." And of Ron Barry, he wrote, "I know of at least two northern experts who consider him to be the greatest jockey now riding over fences. One of them is Guy Cunard, and the other is Harry Bell."

Lord Oaksey, who *did* think Pendil was unlucky, and thought that he had been distracted by the cheering, said that he had never seen fences jumped more brilliantly than

The Dikler jumped the last two; and for him the horse had the authentic "look of eagles" – which is both unmistakable and impossible to define, a mixture of pride and arrogance betrayed by the shape and character of a horse's head.

And Loriner, in his column for *Horse and Hound*, wrote that The Dikler's devouring stride up the straight at Cheltenham had been one of the most inspiring sights that he had ever seen on a racecourse.

Chapter 9

THE WHITBREAD GOLD CUP

THE year after The Dikler had won his Gold Cup his owner received the following invitation from the managing director of the champagne house of Piper Heidsieck, who had been sponsoring the race since 1972:

The Marquis d'Aulan
Requests the pleasure of the company
of
Mrs. D. August

to attend a dinner celebrating the 50th anniversary
of the Cheltenham Gold Cup at The Berkeley,
London, S.W.1. on Wednesday 27th February at
7.30 o'clock.

The youngest Englishwoman present, Peggy August sat beside Fulke Walwyn at the head of one table and listened after dinner to Major General Sir Randle Feilden, Chairman of the Cheltenham Steeplechase Company, tell the guests that the Cheltenham Gold Cup is to National Hunt racing what the King George VI and Queen Elizabeth Stakes at Ascot or the Prix de l'Arc de Triomphe at Longchamp are to flat racing. It was the ultimate proof, he said, of one horse's superiority over all others, and it provided an indisputable champion, being the target of every owner, trainer and jockey. While many jockeys might regard a Grand National victory as more exciting and a greater test of horsemanship, the satisfaction of winning the Cheltenham Gold Cup was, he said, for the owner and trainer anyway, likely to be the realisation of a lifetime ambition. Compared with the King George or the Arc, the rewards were limited; and for a Gold Cup horse there was no prospect of a pampered life at stud. Nor, for the owner of such a horse was there any fortune to come from a harem of mares queuing outside the covering yard. Thanks to the sponsors, however, the actual prize money now represented a more fitting reward than was the case a few years ago. But few owners, said Sir Randle, were motivated by financial considerations when making their entry for the race, and he would hazard a guess that both the £685 won by Red Splash in 1924 and the £15,125 won by The Dikler in 1973, and all the money won in the intervening years, were of secondary importance to the prestige associated with those victories. Sir Randle concluded his speech by saying that, while in terms of prize money National Hunt racing might still be a poor relation to its more affluent flat-racing counterpart, in terms of popular appeal the jumping game was rapidly overhauling flat racing.

The 1972-3 season had been a good one both for Peggy August and Ron Barry. Although Peggy had only one horse in training, she had come fourth in the list of winning owners; while Ron retained his title as Champion Jockey.

The next season was to be another fine one for The Dikler, the chaser who continued to be compulsive watching. True, he could only manage third place in the Massey Ferguson and the King George VI Chase, both of these races being won by Pendil, but in January he came first in the John Bull Chase at Wincanton for the second year running, beating Into View and Kilvulgan; and although this wasn't a spectacular victory, it pleased his jockey, because The Dikler had settled well and done everything that Ron Barry had wanted him to do.

Nine days after his trip to Somerset, The Dikler was up in the North, and one critic wrote that it would be his performance in the John Smith's Great Yorkshire Chase which would tell whether or not he would be a serious rival to Pendil in the 1974 Cheltenham Gold Cup. The Doncaster circuit is pear-shaped, wide and, except for one little hill, dead flat; while the racing surface is so good that it is considered one of the best in the country. It was eminently

Rex Coleman

With Ron Barry up, taken in the yard at Saxon House, Lambourn, two days after winning the 1973 Cheltenham Gold Cup.

suited to a long-striding stayer like The Dikler, and the question now was, could he beat the killer weight of 12 stone 7 lbs. that he had to carry? Ron Barry rode a copybook race on him; and though The Dikler was conceding no fewer than 34 lbs. to Cuckolder, the pair were almost inseparable between the last two fences, and as they came into the straight it became a two-horse race. In the end, The Dikler was unable to beat Mrs. John Rogerson's smart chaser. But in the opinion of John Oaksey, it was a defeat worth more than many victories, for in a fast-run race The Dikler had jumped and galloped magnificently to finish ten lengths ahead of Clever Scot, to whom he was conceding over a stone. Nor was John Oaksey the only journalist who

Ron Barry on The Dikler, when the pair were third in the Massey

Bernard Parkin

thought that The Dikler had run the best race of his career, apart from his triumph in the previous year's Gold Cup.

Burdened by the same weight in his next race, The Dikler conquered it, and the mud, to take the Harwell Handicap Chase at Newbury in February and lift the first prize of £1,103.60. After that, speculation mounted in the Press, and amongst the public, regarding the championship at Cheltenham. Indeed, the return match between The Dikler and Pendil made headlines in more than one paper, and there was endless discussion as to whether Pendil would take his revenge on The Dikler. The other runners seemed virtually to be ignored. A race bringing together two such glamorous horses was a guaranteed box office smash hit; and although Fred Winter's charge was destined never to win this race, he started favourite for it, just as he had done in 1973.

In Lambourn, where a wall stood between their respective stables, the Pendil camp were already hailing this one as the new champion, so impressive had his form been. On the other side of the wall, Fulke Walwyn wisely remarked that nothing is certain in racing when interviewed about his chief contender. But he did tell a reporter, when reviewing his previous Gold Cup winners, the stylish Mont Tremblant, the incredibly game Mandarin and the brilliant jumper Mill House, that The Dikler was the best stayer of the four, and also had the fastest acceleration, besides which he was a horse who really enjoyed his racing.

A few days before the Gold Cup, Peggy August had gone down to Lambourn at 7.30 a.m. to see The Dikler have his final fast gallop, only to be told, "He is cantering today; he decided to do his galloping yesterday."

Ironically, in the light of what was to happen later, Captain Christy, one of two Irish runners in the 1974 Gold Cup, was accorded very little space in the racing columns of the newspapers. His jumping was dismissed as too slapdash, and there was a doubt about his even getting round the course. The other Irish entry was the American-bred

Inkslinger, who had won two races at Cheltenham the previous season, but was not considered a serious threat (except by Peggy, who regarded him as a greater danger than Pendil) because he had not run over this distance. Charlie Potheen had won the Whitbread Gold Cup at Sandown the previous year in amazing style, leading the whole way, treating a welter weight as though it was a feather, and skipping over the last fence to finish five lengths ahead of Colonel Whitbread's Barona. But since then Charlie had had a terrible fall at Newbury, where he turned a somersault, and the chances of this dedicated front-runner were not rated very high. The Queen Mother was represented by Game Spirit, this time the mount of Terry Biddlecombe (Bill Smith was riding Charlie Potheen), but this horse's form was not considered good enough; while the chances of High Ken were rated at 100-1.

So, in most people's minds, it was a question of Pendil or The Dikler, and the former was to start favourite at 13-8 on, with The Dikler at 5-1 and Captain Christy – for whom there was a ton of Irish money – next in demand at 7-1.

"It will be a wonderful spectacle," envisaged Ivor Herbert, "to watch The Dikler, gigantic and jaunty, thundering down that hill, with the dapper little Pendil waiting on him like a winged assassin, waiting until the last. . . ." To a vast majority of racing journalists, the race held promise of a straight duel between two jumping stars; but Tim Fitzgeorge-Parker expressed the opinion that, despite Pendil's four wins in a row, there appeared to be no valid reason why he should be odds on in the ante-post lists to reverse the placings with The Dikler, who had outstayed him and beaten him fair and square up the hill the year before. And he went on to point out that, while Pendil was undoubtedly the best chaser in training over distances up to three miles, in the Great Yorkshire, and in the Harwell Chase, The Dikler had demonstrated that he was back to his brave battling self.

Racing, however, is full of surprises, as well as disappointments, and it was Ireland's Captain Christy, winner of the Irish Sweeps Hurdle at Leopardstown and the Scottish Champion Hurdle at Ayr in the 1972-73 season and trained by Pat Taaffe at Rathcoole in Co. Dublin, who crowned the Irish week at Cheltenham by landing the Cup for Mrs. Jane Samuel from New Zealand. The race was again a dramatic one, with High Ken, who had a reputation for being an unreliable jumper, leading the field until he fell at the third last and brought down Pendil. After the departure of these two, Ron Barry was reluctant to let his horse go ahead so far from home. But he had no choice; and Bobby Beasley, who had kept the Captain in the rear of the field until they came down the hill, then made up so much ground that Captain Christy and The Dikler jumped the final fence almost together. "It was there," said Ron Barry, "that Captain Christy, a very good horse even if he was erratic, made a mistake and I got in front, but he recovered and none of the other horses in the race could have beaten him up the straight. He flew past us, and the best steeplechaser on that day won." The Dikler finished five lengths behind him, but 20 ahead of Game Spirit.

It was a personal triumph for Bobby Beasley, who was winning his second Gold Cup 15 years after he had won his first on Roddy Owen; and he had also won a long battle with the demon alcohol. He confessed afterwards that he found himself schooling Captain Christy in his sleep.

The Beasleys must surely have one of the most remarkable family records in racing. Bobby's great-uncle Tom won the Grand National three times in the 1880's, and once beat Fred Archer in a welter-weight race on the Flat. Bobby's grandfather, Harry Beasley, won the Grand National of 1891 on Come Away, and rode a winner at Punchestown at the age of 68. Bobby himself won the Grand National on Nicolaus Silver in 1961; and his father-in-law, Arthur Thompson, rode two Grand National winners, Sheila's Cottage in 1948 and Teal in 1952.

After the 1974 Gold Cup, Fulke Walwyn wrote to Peggy:

"I think The Dikler is so well that he should aim at the Whitbread. He is really bouncing and came out of the race very well, as you saw. . . ." And Peggy wrote the following letter to Darkie Deacon:–

> Signett Hill,
> Burford,
> Oxon.
>
> March 21st, 1974.
>
> Dear Darkie,
>
> Enclosed is a present for the Gold Cup. Sad the old boy didn't quite make it, but it was a wonderful try. What a pity that they don't have a sportsman's award in that race – both your horses looked superb and I am sure that you'd have won the £25 twice over. I hope Tuppenny will be all right for the Whitbread. I know that he did not perform too well on that course before, but when he's settled that uphill finish should suit him, especially as it should be on top of the ground by then.
>
> Again many thanks for all your work and care.
>
> Yours sincerely,
> Peggy August.

The Whitbread Gold Cup was started by Colonel Bill Whitbread, a great supporter of chasing who had ridden round Aintree as a young man. His idea was to have a valuable handicap steeplechase towards the end of the National Hunt season which would attract horses that had run well at Cheltenham and Liverpool; and he thought, rightly I feel sure, that it would be good publicity for his

firm to promote this. His example was to prove so successful, in fact, that other firms followed it, and National Hunt
prize money swelled to a level which would never have
been achieved without commercial sponsorship. The
Whitbread is run at Sandown over a very fine jumping
course, and it invariably attracts good fields, even though it
is a severe test of stamina, as well as of jockeyship. In the
back straight of the oval right-hand course there are two
lots of fences which come in quick succession, before the
horses are faced with an uphill finish.

That afternoon in the late April of 1974 Ron Barry was
riding with his hand in plaster because he had broken some
bones in it; but Peggy August, who did not care for substi-
tutes, was thankful that The Dikler had Ron on his back.
Like so many others, she has a very high opinion of this
jockey from the North who today lives with his wife and
small son on a hill overlooking Lake Ullswater, describing
him as "full of enthusiasm, bold, yet a great thinker who
makes plans for every race; and if these go astray, soon
adapts to the changed conditions. Over the last mile he
judges just how much he has got left in a horse; so he
knows exactly when to strike."

The Dikler made rather a dodgy start in the Whitbread
but he was in a mood to race – occasionally he was wont to
become what his owner termed flat-footed if he had been
standing in such a manner that the ground was warm
under his size seven plates, and on one occasion at Wincanton he had had to be almost dragged to the post. But once
away at Sandown he was perfectly all right; and as usual,
Ron Barry rode him beautifully despite the plaster cast.

Among the other riders in the race was John Oaksey,
whose reports on racing have been read almost as much for
their wit as for their information ever since he joined the
Daily Telegraph as Marlborough in 1957 and *Horse and Hound*
as Audax in 1959. John's father was, of course, a famous
judge, and John himself had read for the Bar, but became so
interested in horseracing that he was never called to it. The

leading amateur rider in 1957-8, today he was on Sir John Thomson's Proud Tarquin, like The Dikler an 11-year-old, a tough, courageous chaser by Black Tarquin out of Leney Princess. Trained by Roddy Armytage at East Ilsley, Berkshire, he had been second to Red Rum in the Scottish Grand National seven days beforehand.

Before the Whitbread, Lady Thomson had expressed her hope to Peggy that the Cup would stay in their county (Oxfordshire), and it did. For her, however, there was to be a sad end to the race. The Dikler settled well and then worked his way through the field the second time round. "There were three fences in a row, then after the water three more close together, and he seemed to make up ground in the air," recalled Ron. "Going to the last I was challenging John, but Proud Tarquin was a neck in front on landing. Then on the flat he swerved to the left and The Dikler had to veer over, too, or we would have bumped. John immediately straightened his horse but mine had momentarily stopped in his gallop – he immediately went on and was gaining ground on Proud Tarquin when he passed the post, a head behind him."

The favourite, Cuckolder, had set a terrific gallop from the start, accompanied by Credo's Daughter. But he lost ground, through a mistake at the first open ditch on the far side of the course, and faded from the picture after another at the third from home; and it was Inkslinger who deprived Credo's Daughter of third place.

The Stewards had already decided to hold an enquiry before Ron lodged his objection; and after viewing the camera head-on patrol film, they found that Proud Tarquin had interfered with The Dikler. So the placings of the first two were reversed. ("Well at least we know that the Cup will stay in the county," Lady Thomson remarked sportingly to Peggy as they waited for the outcome of the Enquiry.)

The Rules of Racing state that, in the event of an objection, the person making it has to lodge a deposit of £10 which, if the case is decided against him, shall be forfeited to the Jockey Club, unless the Stewards consider that the objection was lodged on reasonable grounds. If they decide it was a "frivolous" or "vexatious" one, they have it in their power to fine the objector any additional sum up to £30. Ron Barry was skint that day, after "too good a night out" with his wife; and to Peggy's amusement, he was obliged to ask Fulke Walwyn if he might borrow the £10 from him!

Looking back on this Whitbread four years later, John Oaksey had nothing but praise for Ron's action when the two of them appeared in front of the Sandown Stewards. "Ron," he says, "was very nice about it, and he did nothing to make it sound worse than it was – which is what some jockeys will try to do in such circumstances. But the Stewards did decide that there was interference – I had only won by a head. Perhaps, though, it was a pity that only one of the three had any experience of jumping. Proud Tarquin had been known before to hang in finishes, and in the Whitbread I had my whip in my left hand and I hit him down the neck to straighten him out. The Dikler saw him coming and swerved away from the threat. Arguably, I was unlucky to be disqualified because the two horses didn't actually bump each other; but it was a very good performance by The Dikler, who was giving my horse a lot of weight." A stone and 10 lbs., in fact.

On May 1st, 1974, Lady Thomson posted the following letter:–

Woodperry House,
Woodperry,
Oxon.

Dear Mrs. August,

We were so touched and did so appreciate your letter. If we had to lose the race we were glad that it was to such a wonderful horse and to such nice owners. Naturally we were sad, especially for John and Roddy and for the yard. Nevertheless, that is what racing is all about and one takes the rough with the smooth. We went to see 'Tarky' on Sunday and he looked as though he had never had a race, and today he is eating his summer grass, but I am afraid not in summer weather. Again thank you for your nice letter,

Yours sincerely,
Edith Thomson.

This letter shows that both horses had owners to be proud of; and on May 20th, Peggy August wrote again to The Dikler's lad at Saxon House:–

Dear Darkie,

Thank you again for all the time and energy that you have spent on 'Tuppenny'. I am just so pleased that he was able to reward you with that fine win at Sandown (what a pity that the old boy did not get the pleasure of knowing that he'd won!). I gather from John [Honeyball] that he is quite settled at Attington, and though he went out looking grand I guess he will have gained a cwt. already. I hope you have a good summer with plenty of golf. Tony Jacklin was playing at Burford a fortnight ago, so you must give it a try and see what you think of the course. Enclosed is a cheque which I have much pleasure in sending you.

Yours sincerely,
Peggy August.

Chapter 10

THE DIKLER AT AINTREE

ALTHOUGH the 1974 Whitbread Gold Cup was the last race The Dikler was to win, it was by no means the end of his racing career; and at the back of Fulke Walwyn's mind there was always the Grand National for him, a race that Peggy August had been holding out against for some time; not because she believed that the big fences would trouble her horse, but because of the hazards from loose horses, who might bring him down. Eventually she came round. This is how she puts it:

"I suppose I got to know Fulke quite well; and when, in the New Year, he started calling me 'Darling' I knew that 'What about the National?' was coming next. Fulke generally knew what the answer to this would be, so I didn't actually have to say no. More often than not, we would just have a giggle together. But eventually I said yes, because I had begun to feel that, at 12, which he then was, The Dikler, would find the Cheltenham Gold Cup beyond him; and he seemed to be given so much weight in all the other handicaps. Also I felt that it was Fulke's ambition to win another National – he had won it in 1964 with Team Spirit, who was also by Vulgan – and I knew that it would please him if The Dikler at least had a go. I also felt that Fulke knew that I would just about shoot him if anything happened to the horse. So he would not have suggested it unless he was confident that, barring an accident, The Dikler would jump his way round safely."

The Dikler had his first race of the 1974-75 season in the Hennessy Gold Cup at Newbury, where he was without his usual jockey, as Ron Barry was out of action with an injured wrist and a broken bone in his arm. However, Aly Branford was able to settle The Dikler, and the horse ran pretty well under his big weight until he got bogged down in the home straight after moving up to within striking distance of the leaders along the back straight on the second circuit, eventually finishing sixth to the bottom weight, Royal Marshal II.

He was fifth in the Massey Ferguson at Cheltenham, where Ron Barry was back in the saddle, and fourth to the lowly-weighted Moonlight Escapade in the Mandarin Chase at Newbury, where he started a hot favourite, despite the presence in the field of Cuckolder and Proud Tarquin. At Newbury, he was trying to give the winner more than 2 stone, as well as conceding lumps of weight to the others. The race was run at a slow pace for the first two miles and it was clear that he was taking an even stronger hold than usual. Besides this, he pulled a muscle in his quarters, and Darkie Deacon said afterwards that he thought he detected signs of lameness. Indeed, intermittent lameness was to create problems for his trainer later and cause him to put the horse on the easy list.

He was, however, to have two more races before the Grand National, being pulled up before the twelfth in the Cheltenham Gold Cup won by Ten Up, and finishing down the field in a handicap chase at Newbury run in very heavy going.

Doubts were expressed in the Press as to whether the muscular trouble he had been having would cause him to miss the National; but when it became known that he had responded well to therapeutic treatment, there was considerable excitement. Robin Goodfellow in the *Daily Mail* expressed the opinion that the Aintree course must have been constructed with such a horse as The Dikler in mind; and another paper described him as a colourful character who inspired both devotion and criticism. He did, of course, have his detractors, who insisted that he would be better pulling a barge along the canal than jumping the fences. But there were also those who maintained that the Vulgan-sired veteran could stage a champion run on his first visit to Aintree; including, no doubt, the 13-year-old fan who wrote to Fulke Walwyn wishing him and The

Dikler good luck, and saying, "I shall be glued to the television screen to watch the National to fulfil my dream of seeing The Dikler run in it." A Scottish fan, to whom Fulke had given a photograph of The Dikler, sent him a sprig of white heather as a good-luck token for the big race.

Darkie Deacon left Lambourn with The Dikler the day before the race. The Dikler's travelling companion was Zellaman, who was running in a hurdle race on the same day as the National (and was to finish third in it). "I stayed in the racecourse hostel," Darkie told me, "and The Dikler was bedded down in the warmest box I could find for him – he always had the miseries in strange places."

Peggy August had stayed in Liverpool with friends and only went to Aintree for the race. "I was with Fulke in the Duke of Devonshire's box, and Jimmy Tarbuck the comedian sat on my other side. I always got so tense when my horse was running, wherever the race was, and I shut my eyes as usual for most of the circuits. Jimmy was telling jokes that went right over my head, and said to Fulke, 'All my wisecracks are wasted on your owner.' "

Peggy did, however, watch her horse jump the formidable Chair fence; and it was here that he produced one of his finest jumps. "We thought," she said, "that he might lose ground at the Canal Turn, but he jumped it neatly, despite his muscular trouble."

This was the National that Red Rum was attempting to win for the third year in succession, and in which he went under to L'Escargot. The Dikler galloped and fenced magnificently, and Darkie was only sorry that some of his most spectacular leaps were out of range of the camera, since The Dikler's negotiation of them completely refuted those people who were saying he was but a shadow of his former self. Glanford Brig had been sharing the lead with Southern Quest on the second circuit, and when he began to show signs of strain from four fences out it was The Dikler who looked to be going the best of all; and it was not until the third last that his big weight of 11 st. 13 lbs. started to tell on him. Even so, it was only on the flat after the last fence that he was overtaken for fourth place by Money Market; and of those horses who finished in front of him, only Red Rum was carrying more weight.

After the race, Fulke Walwyn received the following letter from a young admirer in Enfield, Middlesex:–

Dear Mr. Walwyn,

I am asking a favour of you. Would it be possible for me to have a photo of The Dikler, my favourite horse? He ran so well in the Grand National, how unfair to give him all that weight. He should have been third or fourth. Does he like polo mints?

The Dikler began what was to be his last season in the Old Year Handicap Chase at Cheltenham on the eve of his official 13th birthday, December 31st, 1975. He was giving 21 lbs. to Floating Pound and more than 2 stone to Sonny Somers; and for a moment he looked like catching them both going up the hill he knew so well, only to fail gallantly by a length and a neck. It was his first public appearance for eight months.

He had four more races before essaying the Cheltenham Gold Cup again. In the first of them, a race he was expected to walk, the 2½-mile Partridge Chase at Chepstow, he ran unaccountably badly and was beaten eight lengths by Soloning, a horse who hadn't had a race since breaking down two years ago. He then ran, some two weeks later, in the Gainsborough Chase at Sandown, where he finished a respectable second to Bula, who started at 3-1 on.

His next race was the Whitbread Trial Handicap Chase at Ascot, where, with Bill Smith deputising for the injured Ron Barry, he refused altogether to race. His last race before Cheltenham in March was the Jim Ford Cup at Wincanton, where, reunited with Ron Barry, he was third to Summerville and Eyecatcher.

In the Gold Cup, with Aly Branford riding him, he was going very well until he ruined his chances by taking off outside the wing at the top of the hill on the final circuit, eventually finishing eighth to Royal Frolic. "We had the National in mind then," said his owner, "and had put him in the Gold Cup because we considered that it was the best preparation for him, as a true, fast-run race at level weights was calculated to take much less out of him than giving away lumps of weight in another handicap would have done."

On The Dikler's last visit to Aintree, Peggy August arrived at the course at 7 a.m. "Most of the horses out for exercise," she said, "were being cantered; but I knew that Darkie was only going to give our horse walking exercise in the paddock – we dared not let him go on the course in case he took off. When I got to the stables there was a security man standing in front of the door of The Dikler's box (which had once been used by Foinavon), and I asked him, 'Is The Dikler in or out? I am his owner.' All he said was, 'I am not here to answer questions like that.' "

The 1976 Grand National was the one won by Rag Trade from Red Rum and Eyecatcher. The Dikler was set to carry 11 st. 7 lbs. in it, as against Rag Trade's 10 st. 12 lbs. and Red Rum's 11 st. 10 lbs. Ridden once again by Ron Barry, he was well up with the leaders for the greater part of the journey, pulling his jockey's arms out; but once again he didn't quite get the trip, though until the last half-mile he looked as though he would be in the money. In the end, he finished sixth.

Would he, in his prime, ever have won this great race? When I asked Ron Barry this question at his home in the Lake District, he answered that he, personally, did not think so. "There were," he said, "too many horses in it, and too many distractions; and with me," he added, "he never settled, never relaxed. He was always fighting for his head and using up his energy. But over the fences he gave me a super ride both times."

On the occasion of the 1976 Grand National, all the horses who had won a classic race were riven a large red, white and blue rosette with the name of the races inscribed on the centre of it. Most wore the rosettes on their browbands; but when Fulke Walwyn said that he thought this would make The Dikler look like a beast in a fat-stock market, Peggy carried his rosette herself. She was, she said, trembling so much with this in her hand that Ron looked at her and said with a grin, "What the hell are you shaking for? It's me who's going to ride the race, not you."

Although Peggy August's horse didn't win any prize money, the thrill of taking The Dikler to Aintree again had been well worth it; and the race proved that age had dimmed neither his courage nor his love of the game.

From a Norfolk admirer, Fulke Walwyn received the following letter:–

> Dear Mr. Walwyn,
>
> How splendidly The Dikler ran in this year's Grand National. I watched the race twice, in the afternoon at 3.15 and again at midnight on T.V. I felt terribly sad when I realised that I might never see him race again because of his age – it will seem as though a light has gone out of my life.

And a Hampshire one wrote this:–

> Dear Mr. Walwyn,
>
> Last year I wrote to congratulate you on the running of The Dikler in the Grand National. Once again I am writing to congratulate you and Ron Barry on his performance this year. If anything had happened to him I think it would have broken my heart.

Chapter 11

THE DIKLER IN RETIREMENT

TOWARDS the end of the 1975-76 season Peggy August and Fulke Walwyn both began to feel, independently of each other, that the time was fast drawing near when The Dikler should go into happy retirement. Neither of them wanted to see him slowly sliding down the scale and being beaten by lesser horses. They felt he deserved the honour of departing from the scene while he was still at the top. "Suddenly," said Peggy, "we were both talking about the Whitbread being his last race before retirement."

And that's how it was. "Hail and Farewell" was one of the headlines after the 1976 Whitbread Gold Cup, in which Otter Way, who, like The Dikler, started his racing career in point-to-points, imprinted his mark on the N.H. scene. The Dikler, a horse getting on for twice his age, put up a brave display to finish fourth, eight lengths ahead of Red Rum. Both these great horses were giving weight away to all those who finished in front of them.

So the horse whose fan mail, it is said, has been the largest of any chaser since the War, with the exception of Arkle and Red Rum, had run his last race. In a published letter, Martin Lord summed up his racing career in these words: "Historically his record was impressive. Few horses have won the King George VI Chase, the Cheltenham Gold Cup and the Whitbread Gold Cup in their lifetime. But it is not for this that I and other racegoers will remember him. He had something special, something that attracted people and won their hearts. He was a brilliant jumper who put everything into the game; and if at times he behaved like a naughty, overgrown schoolboy, it only seemed in keeping with his incredible character."

The Dikler was, of course, fortunate in the people who looked after him and had his welfare at heart. He had an owner who, while never sentimental about him, put his

The Dikler's owner, Mrs Peggy Boddington (formerly Mrs August), holding her champion, with her

value beyond money. In John Honeyball and Darkie
Deacon he had two wonderful mentors; and in Ron Barry,
the quiet Irishman who rode him in his finest hour, and
twice completed the Grand National on him, an immensely
skilful horseman and intuitive jockey.

Above all, there was Fulke Walwyn, that master of his
profession who trained him to become one of the greatest
steeplechasers in England; and whose wife, Cath (*née* de
Trafford), works so tirelessly to help him. In the words of
Peggy August, "Cath Walwyn is totally aware of all that
goes on in the yard at Saxon House and knows and
appreciates the high standards that are required there, as
well as being invaluable at relieving the strain at race meetings on big occasions."

In 1974, when David August died from a heart attack at
the age of 44, Peggy was left to run, not only Signett Farm,
but also that belonging to her mother, who lives just up the
road from her. The shock of her husband's death, combined with the extra work, diminished even Peggy's seem-
ingly inexhaustible energy; and her friends and family were
much relieved when, two years later she married Myles
Boddington, who owns Waterloo Farm on the other side of
Burford.

Peggy remembers how sad she felt when she and her
stepdaughter, Jackie Boddington, went to collect The
Dikler from Lambourn for the last time. "Darkie had got
him up looking a picture, and I knew that I could never
expect to own another racehorse like him, and doubted
whether I should ever have a racehorse again. So I was
virtually saying good-bye to Saxon House. As I was about
to get into the box, Fulke put his hand on my shoulder,
looked me straight in the eye, and said, 'Take good care of
him. He has been a good friend.'" He was, she said, "near
to tears as The Dikler was driven out through the gates of
Saxon House."

Fulke had suggested to Peggy that she ought to have The
Dikler as a hunter, following the horse's retirement from

the racecourse. "He'd never stop, you know," he told her.

"I know," Peggy had responded. "That is what I would be afraid of." So she offered The Dikler to Jackie, a very able event rider, to do what she liked with the horse whose legs were as clean and hard as on the day when he ran in his first point-to-point.

"I'll have a go and see how we get on," Jackie replied. Her idea was to ride him in hunter trials, as well as hunting him; and he now spends his winters at Waterloo Farm, where Jackie lives with her sisters, and his summer with Peggy at Signett Farm.

Contrary to reports that he was a menace to other horses in the field, The Dikler has always been so safe with them that Peggy had no qualms about turning him out with shoes on; and her mother, Mrs. Ernest Bee, remembers how he used to follow her about like a dog when he was out at grass in the days before he went to Lambourn. (When he was first turned out on his return from Saxon House he had been given an injection to prevent him from galloping about too much, and the vet prescribed such a big one, on account of his size, that he was rendered comatose for almost a week.)

Since Peggy keeps some of her hunters at Waterloo Farm, and rides out from there, she has been able to see The Dikler most days; and when he is being got fit in the autumn, she often exercises him herself. On the road, he is so good with traffic – like a police horse, Jackie says – that he is always put on the outside of his stable companions, or in front of them; and when hacking, they can lead a horse off him.

Jackie Boddington was determined to start at the bottom with The Dikler, and get him completely settled in his new way of life. The first season she had him, he was given pony cubes and very few oats. To begin with, Jackie rode him about the farm. He never once tried to run away with her, or rear or buck, she says, "but he would whip round when I wanted him to leave the yard by himself. So for a time I could not go for a ride on my own, because he was so used to having other horses with him; but after a while he did not mind being alone with me." Jackie had ridden many different types of horse, and encountered many different temperaments; but none in the least like The Dikler, she says. She found him a challenge.

After leaving Saxon House for good, The Dikler was first hunted with the Heythrop by Charles Vernon Miller, the trainer, who told Peggy, on dismounting, that he felt "more famous now" than when he had won the Hennessy Gold Cup with one of his horses.

Shortly after this, The Dikler had a recurrence of his old muscular trouble and was laid up for a couple of months – they always knew when he was in pain, because he dragged his foot and wore down one side of his shoe. But Jackie was able to hunt him several times herself that season, and a well-known jockey who saw him expressed his surprise at the horse's impeccable behaviour at gateways.

In March 1977, The Dikler was taken to David Hunt, the dressage instructor, along with Jackie's event horses, since there was a spare stall in the box and it was felt that he might just as well go too. I asked Peggy how he got on with his lessons, and she replied that his trot was good, but he could not resist looking at himself in the mirror – a feature of all indoor schools – while Jackie was to find that he had difficulty cantering to the left, because he always struck off on the right leg.

Three days after his visit to David Hunt, The Dikler came fourth at an indoor jumping show, with only four faults in his two rounds. "Neither of us had done this before," said Jackie, "yet whatever you put him at he jumped."

At the end of March the pair were competing indoors again, and this time The Dikler came first in the jumping, but was relegated to fourth place overall in this combined training event after an explosive dressage test. "He thought, when doing the dressage test," said Jackie, "that he was going to jump. So he was cantering most of the time, and once we'd cantered he was not interested in any other pace."

At the beginning of April, the V.W.H. hunter trials were held, and here The Dikler missed out a string jump which his rider considered too flimsy for him. "It was dangerous," Jackie said, "because he couldn't see it – I could hardly do so myself." Later that month he went to stay with David Hunt for two days, while Jackie was eventing at Windsor; and the instructor told Peggy that had her horse not been a top steeplechaser he could have been a top dressage horse. In fact, as I write this, he is practising the counter canter.

At the Evenlode Riding Club spring show that season he won both the veterans' class and the hunter championship, giving the judge a perfect ride. Unfortunately, he then blotted his copybook by proving too strong in the dressage test; and as Jackie had no time to change his noseband, he simply "took off" in the jumping and galloped out of the ring. But as though to make amends for this intransigent behaviour, he did a good collected dressage test at the Oxford Show; and in May I watched him take part in the celebrity parade at the Bath & West. This happened to take place on the same day that Prince Charles honoured the show with his presence. The Dikler, who likes a Royal occasion as much as anyone else, paraded sedately before the Prince of Wales; and then, not wanting to move away with the other horses after the line-up, he was left standing by himself in front of the Royal Box, and remained there until Jackie's sister, Sally, who works for Alison Oliver (Princess Anne's trainer), ran into the ring and led him on.

During the pre-parade at this show, a man standing next to Peggy wondered out loud, "What lunatic put that young girl up on The Dikler?" Peggy then admitted responsibility, and "tried to assure him that the horse and rider knew each other well enough to prevent a disaster."

"The afternoon had started off all right," Jackie told me, "but then we had to wait a long time for a jumping competition to finish, and The Dikler never has liked waiting about; and after some photographs had been taken, he was alternately stopping and starting. I feared that he might be going to be difficult – I can generally sense when he is – but, thank goodness, there was one horse in front of him and he walked round two circuits of the big ring perfectly, except for a half-stop in the bottom corner. I was riding short and he was in a snaffle, so I had nothing to help me with him. Then, when we were all lined up in front of the Royal Box, he evidently thought that this was the start of something, because he was jumping up and down. When the others moved off, however, he declined to do so. So I signalled to my sister, who was ready waiting to come to my aid; and after she had led him for a few steps, away he went to catch up with the parade."

The Dikler's holiday at Signett Farm that year was cut short owing to the flies which were bothering him so much in the field; and in September he was helping to raise money for the Injured Jockeys' Fund at Woburn. It so happened that Jackie had parked her horse-box at the side of the ring – something that she would not have done had she known what was coming. After the commentary on each horse was finished, some small jumps were brought into the ring, and John Oaksey, the organiser, then invited the riders to take their horses over them. The Dikler jumped the one nearest the box; and then, when he realised that he was not going back to his box, could not be persuaded to take any further part in the entertainment. "However," said Peggy, "Dick Pitman could not persuade Crisp over any of the jumps. So we were not too depressed." After the show, Peggy received the following letter from John Oaksey:–

Dear Mrs. Boddington,

Thank you so much for letting The Dikler come to Woburn the other day. Considering

> that we made £1,000 for the Injured Jockeys'
> Fund it was a fairly painless afternoon.
> Please thank Jackie for riding so beautifully –
> I really do admire the way she has come to
> terms with The Dikler's foibles.

The big horse attended a few more hunter trials before he started hunting again, only to jump on an iron stake. This held him up for weeks, but Jackie had some good days with him after that. "Although out hunting I sometimes have to go to the front quicker than I want to, I do not as a rule let him gallop as fast as he would like, as it is too tiring for me, though I now get less exhausted than I did." She hunts him in boots since he marked his leg through an over-reach. Never once, incidentally, did he race in bandages; and to date he has had only one fall, and that through no fault of his own.

Both Peggy and Jackie hunt with the farmers on Mondays and Fridays; and on the day that the accident happened, Peggy was riding Gail, a horse who was a ferocious bucker until re-educated by John Honeyball. "We came to a set of rails," said Jackie, "and I thought that I had given Peggy plenty of room to jump them. So I sailed over, not knowing that there was a ditch about three strides away. Gail came to a grinding halt at it, and Tuppenny took two strides straight into the back of her; and when Gail was just about to jump the ditch, there was no room for Tuppeny, who was already in the air – he had his forelegs round Peggy's neck, or so it seemed to me – and as there was no way round, he fell into the gully head first and pitched me onto the bank the other side. He was absolutely outraged at what had happened to him, and when he got out he galloped off across a sticky ploughed field. I had an awful job going after him in my riding boots; and though a man kindly caught him for me, he would not be led back. Eventually, I had to get up on him from the floor – at home I mount from walls or dustbins – but he stood quietly until I managed to climb into the saddle."

Jackie is another person who will tell you that The Dikler is a lovely horse to ride because he is so beautifully balanced and light on his feet; and she feels very honoured to have him in her yard. In his box, she says, he is affectionate and reasonably co-operative; and she is intrigued by the way he notices everything, and takes a keen interest in what is going on around him. When some men were cutting down old elm trees half a mile away from the stables, he spent hours watching them. "The Dikler," says Jackie, "is a great character with a will of his own; and even out hunting he will stand stock-still in the middle of a field, and nothing you can do will get him to go on until he is ready to do so."

Ever since Waterloo Farm has been The Dikler's second home, Peggy and her stepdaughter have found that an outing about once a week in the horse-box or trailer has a beneficial effect on him. "We call these his parties," says Peggy, "and he does enjoy the change. If he is not taken somewhere he becomes a bit cheeky in the stable and needs tying up short while being groomed." Sarah Stanton, the smiling girl groom, has little trouble using the body brush on him. "He is ticklish in several places," she says, "but I know where they are." As she told me this, she was holding The Dikler's tail while he stood still in his box; and it is obvious that she is as devoted to her massive charge as John Honeyball and Darkie Deacon were in days gone by.

Among the letters received at Lambourn and Signett Farm after The Dikler's retirement was this one from Sarah Waugh of Guildford:–

Dear Darkie Deacon,

My mother and I are great fans of The Dikler. We saw him run in the Whitbread Gold Cup and took lots of photos of him. My mother is always talking about him to her friends. She is very proud that she patted him when you brought him out of the stable for her. She does not know that I am writing to you, but I wonder if you could tell me how he is? My mother followed him from the start of his racing career when he was point-to-pointing to his retirement. Will we see him in point-to-points again? I hope so because I know that all over England there are many fans of this great horse . . .

And from N. Lake of Plymouth, Darkie had this letter:–

I feel it is only right that you should be thanked for what you have done for The Dikler. Ever since he emerged on the racing scene he has been the number one character. He leaves racing the same way as he came in – by stealing the imagination, and now that he has gone he has left an unfillable vacuum. I hope he gets as much pleasure out of retirement as I got out of watching him. Thank you again, and I would also like to thank Mr. Walwyn for all he has done. Lesser men, I am sure, would have broken the horse's spirit during his somewhat wayward youth.

For Adrian Gregory, a student at the University of Kent, The Dikler opened up a wonderful world of horseracing and gave him a passionate interest in the National Hunt scene. "From the moment I first saw The Dikler when he beat Bannons Star," he wrote, "I felt so dedicated to him that I felt I owned him," while to J.G. Richardson "his retirement was the end of an era" and after he had watched the horse's last race on television "the whole racing scene suddenly became empty without him."

The Dikler, it would seem, "belonged" to everybody.

The horse nobody would buy when he was for sale in England imprinted his name on a sparkling era, and no star has arisen to take his place in the heart of the racing public.

Index